SECRET SKILL HIDDEN CAREER

The surprising link between sales ability and your career success

PAUL OWEN

RETHINK PRESS

First published in Great Britain 2017

by Rethink Press (www.rethinkpress.com)

Contents

Foreword

When I was first introduced to Paul, he told me about his programme to introduce people to sales as a life skill and a career and I was struck by his passion and his resolve as well as the common sense behind what he said. We all sell in our lives and yet we don't teach this skill in schools, colleges or universities. If anything, we discourage people from learning the skill of selling because of the negative connotation it has in our culture. It's bizarre to think that this critical skill remains the secret of the few and that the career/life it offers is hidden to most people looking for a job. I don't think Paul is alone in recognising this problem but he was the first person I'd met who'd resolved to put selling as the number one skill any individual can have.

I was delighted when he told me about his plans to extend the educational programme to write this book and flattered that he asked me to write this foreword.

I have enjoyed my life so far, achieving goals across the wheel of life, whether that's been in my work life, my success in the sports and charity sectors, the honour of several awards, my role as a husband or father, or enjoying some great experiences through travel and wonderful friendships. In achieving my goals, there is a common success factor – and that is selling!

Anybody who has been in business for a few years knows that the ability to communicate messages in a compelling way is one of the most important skills in the workplace. Whether it's talking to customers, to colleagues, to managers or to your own teams, we all need to sell our ideas to people. We do that first by understanding them, by listening to them. I was delighted to see that Paul's book devotes two whole chapters to the skill of asking great questions and listening to the answers. Without that, it's impossible to advise people, which is effectively what selling is: well-informed advice.

If you were to look at my career, you won't see sales in any of my job titles, yet my roles in customer service, leadership and strategy have all incorporated the ability to communicate effectively, and it's fair to say that this is selling.

As a career, sales is not for everyone. However, with at least 3 million people employed in sales in the UK right now, it is an area that is at least worth knowing about before you decide. As a skill, sales is for everyone. Whatever job you do, whatever life you lead, you will have a higher chance of success if you master this skill. Done well, it's about helping people. Don't think of it as pressure, as talking at people, of forcing others to think what you think and buy what you're selling. Humans are too smart for that to work effectively and consistently.

In Paul, you couldn't have a better guide to your introduction to this skill and career. For some of you, this book will change your life.

Whatever it is you do in life from this point, I wish you well. Carpe Diem.

Chris Brindley

FOREWORD

Chris Brindley is one of the UK's foremost business leaders. Until August 2015, he served as Managing Director of Metro Bank, which opened its doors to the public in 2010. Since then the bank has grown rapidly and it is already recognised as the top challenger to its highly established, powerhouse competitors. Chris is now an Executive Coach and Mentor for business leaders throughout the UK. A renowned keynote speaker across the world, Chris chairs one of the UK's leading charities, GreaterSport, and is a Non-Executive Director of Rugby Football League and Manchester Football Association, as well as a range of other sporting bodies and independent businesses.

Introduction

A life-changing decision

November 2000, London

At the age of thirty-two, I was £26,000 in debt and earning £8,000 a year in a data admin job which gave me no life skills, no career opportunity and no self-esteem. Nine credit card statements arrived on my doorstep each month. The girl with whom I'd recently fallen in love had left me because of the state I was in. I was living for free in a friend's small back bedroom. Despite having such kind friends and a supportive family, I had never thought my life would turn out like this.

On 5 December 2000, I got a new job. It was a sales job, the kind of role I'd dismissed for years as something for people less able than me. However, it changed my life. I loved it. Four years later, I earned my first ever annual bonus, taking my total earnings that year to more than £100,000.

The point of this story is not to show you my brilliance but my stupidity. I was nothing special, but once I let go of my ignorance and snobbery about sales, I went from being broke to being very well paid and loving my job.

You don't need to make the mistakes I made, you don't need to end up in the position I did, but you may need some help to take the next step. That's what this book is about.

I'd like to teach you to sell, persuade, influence, communicate well. These skills are arguably the most important ones you will ever learn. In any career, you will need them. Do them well and you're more likely to be successful. Not only will they help your career, I have no doubt they will help your personal life too.

The great shame is that people aren't taught how to sell. This life-critical skill is not taught in schools, colleges or universities. It's not available at job centres or any other place people turn for career skills. I know because I've been to many of them and asked.

This shortfall in skills training is a blind spot that I have been known to call a national tragedy, a disgrace, a shocking omission from our education system and our culture. It's all of those things and more.

Sales is possibly the largest function in business. If a company fails to persuade people to buy its services and products, it fails. Simple. If it succeeds in selling, it has a better than average chance of success.

This book is my attempt to open people's eyes to the skill of sales. I hope my passion for it will shine through these pages. I hope it helps every reader to do sales better. Where that will take you, nobody knows, but I remain convinced that the best business apprenticeship is a few years in sales. The career it offers should not be hidden from so many people.

First, I'd like to debunk a whole range of myths about sales, because it was those myths that stopped me from considering a job in sales. Then I'll give you ten great reasons to consider sales as an early step in your career, whatever you choose to do later, and highlight the attributes you'll need to do it well. Once you understand what sales really is and why it might interest you, I'm going to teach you how to sell in a way that will see clients return to you again and again because they trust you. Selling done properly is about helping people make good buying decisions. I'll show you how to do that consistently and ethically.

Finally, you'll discover how many different career paths are available to people who have developed their communication skills to a high level. Two to five years in a sales job not only earns you good money but also teaches you skills that can be applied to any number of lucrative and exciting careers. Dotted throughout this book are real-life stories of successful business people who have either started in sales or built a significant part of their success on their ability to sell. I hope their stories will inspire you.

This book is aimed at anyone looking for career guidance and improved skills. If you don't go into sales, you'll still be better equipped to do well in any field. If sales becomes an option by the end, you'll be well-informed and well-prepared for your first steps. I want this book to change thousands of lives, but a friend reminded me that if it changes just one life for the better, I can be proud of the time I put into it.

I hope that life is yours.

Paul Owen, 2017

How To Read This Book

I present sales skills in a training format in this book as that's the best way to bring them to life. Although you can't just read this book and be trained in sales, you will gain a much better understanding of what's involved and a clear idea of what to do next. As you go through the training sections, read them as if you're reading any other book. If, after reading the whole book, you want to take notes and put ideas into practice, go back to the relevant sections, but I wouldn't advise doing that on the first reading. Enjoy the book first.

The real life-stories found throughout the book will show you where great sales skills can take you in life, from the Geography graduate who learnt his trade selling records and went on to become the Chief Operating Officer of the London Olympics, to the young girl who turned to sales when her father went bankrupt and later sold her company for £20 million, giving her the choice to retire at forty.

Finally, at various times in the book, I ask you to do things. Please do them before you read on. I'd like my book to be a conversation between you and me, so your participation will help it work as well as possible.

CHAPTER 1

Secrets, Myths And Scandal

'Everybody makes a living by selling something.'
ROBERT LOUIS STEVENSON

Society tends to look down upon sales and I'm still not entirely sure why. I've asked many people and they tell me it's because there are dishonest salespeople or salespeople who force you to buy things you neither want nor need. That is true in some cases, but there are the dishonest and unethical in every walk of life. Scandal and corruption has hit many other areas, from professional footballers and Olympic athletes to car manufacturers and journalists, but they're not ruined by it. So why is 'sales' tarnished?

The prevailing belief is that salespeople just want to sell you something to make money and will lie or exaggerate to do so. They don't care if you're happy or not. Who'd want to be a salesperson? Who'd want to lie all the time? What a horrible way to live!

There is a range of myths surrounding sales skills and sales as a job. As the main aim of this book is to share the truth about sales, I'd like to start by shattering these myths.

- Sales Myth 1: selling is about talking at people all the time
- Sales Myth 2: nobody likes being sold to because they hate salespeople
- Sales Myth 3: sales is a rubbish job with no career prospects.

There are more myths but these three are the real killers of an interest in sales as both a skill and a career. We'll attack them one by one.

Shattering Sales Myth 1: selling is about talking at people all the time. When I run my company's communication programmes at schools, colleges and universities, I ask the participants to do an exercise before I address the myths around sales. If you're the courageous sort, try the following challenge, either in your head or out loud, as if you're working with someone on it. It may feel strange, but it will make what you're about to learn more useful.

Challenge: imagine yourself working with a partner. One of you is a potential buyer and the other is the salesperson. The salesperson chooses a product or service they'd like to sell – to keep it simple, choose something you can see (a chair, desk, bag, coat, etc.). He or she then has sixty seconds to convince the buyer that this is the greatest chair/desk/bag in the world and it's worth every penny of their money. How could they possibly resist? At the end of sixty seconds, change roles, with buyer becoming salesperson and vice versa.

Start the clock and sell away!

How was it for you? When I ask for feedback from programme participants at the end of the sixty-second sales pitches, both buyer and seller in most cases will say it was hard to do. Here's what usually happens.

The seller talks and talks. They run out of content somewhere between the twenty and thirty-five second point, so repeat what they've already said or demonstrate their ability to convey the exact same meaning while using different words. Or changed vocabulary. Or alternative phraseology. A bit like I've just done.

As for the potential buyers, they process very little of what the seller actually says. Largely, it becomes 'Blah, blah, blah… '

Because people normally do the exercise with a friend, it tends to be more relaxed and pleasant than it would be in the real world. In reality, when someone approaches us to sell something by telling us how amazing it is, what do we do? Most of us are just waiting for them to draw breath so that we can jump in and say, 'I'm not interested, thanks.' Phew, got rid of them.

At that moment, if we were asked what the salesperson had been selling to us, our answer would likely be, 'I don't know.' Why? Because when we're sold to in that way, we switch off from the message and our mind wanders elsewhere. Must pick up some milk on way home. Wonder if that party will be good tonight.

This is not the right way to sell because it's not the way we like to buy things. We don't like people we don't know telling us that a product or service will change our lives – they cannot possibly know this and so the message has no credibility and, consequently, no real audience.

So, what is sales? Selling – when done properly – is helping people make good buying decisions. You cannot do that by talking at people when you know nothing about them. We buy many of the same products and services as each other, but we buy them for different reasons. A salesperson cannot sell the same products to different people in the same way.

So selling is about helping customers, and this means you must take time to listen to them and understand them. Only then can you advise them.

Depending on the product and sector, it is possible to become a good salesperson by being a good talker. But you'll only become a great salesperson – or a great communicator in any field – by being a good listener. Take yourself back to being a buyer. Wouldn't you prefer to buy from someone who listens to you and takes time to understand you? Someone who tailors what they offer to match your individual needs?

In summary, selling is not about talking at people all the time. Selling, done properly, is helping people make good buying decisions by listening to them and understanding their needs. I particularly want you to challenge the widespread acceptance of Sales Myth 1 because it's the root of the other two myths.

Shattering Sales Myth 2: nobody likes being sold to because they hate salespeople. Interpreted in a certain way, this myth could be true. But that certain way is the wrong way.

Let me explain.

We love being sold to. I promise, we really do. We just don't like being sold to in the way I described in the exercise above. We don't like being talked at, lectured, closed in sixty seconds by an assumptive, over-confident sales pitch during which we have no input. But it's different if we trust the person selling to us; if they're professional, credible, likeable; if they take time to understand us first and only sell us something relevant and interesting that solves problems we have.

When we're buyers, we're usually idiots. I'm an idiot in almost every buying decision I make. By idiot, I mean that I know far less about the products I'm buying than the person selling them to me.

Of course, as the buyer, I feel like I should be the whole focus of the conversation. But I shouldn't be in charge. When I visit my doctor, the conversation is all about me, but I don't control the conversation. The doctor does. They ask the questions, they direct the subject matter. I let them lead because I trust them to know a lot more than I do about my health.

Great salespeople make buyers feel the same way great doctors do. They build trust. They take time to understand people. They make their recommendations – like a doctor makes a diagnosis – based on the information they've learnt about you, and they offer a solution that solves your problem and helps you feel better. In order to do that, they have to build trust, and once they have that, they will help you make good buying decisions.

I'd like to tell you a true story about a cobbler in London. Though good at mending shoes, he didn't recognise that buyers want to take advice from a trusted expert and, through that, he lost my custom.

I took two pairs of shoes to him a few years ago. They were quite expensive shoes and, after I'd worn them for a few weeks, a friend had advised me to take them to a cobbler who could strengthen them, making them more durable.

My conversation with the cobbler – let's call him Joe – went something like this:

'Hi, Joe. A mate of mine told me that I should get these shoes protected to make them last longer. I think he said something about getting extra soles put on and the heels strengthened. He may have said that the leather can have a coating on too. What do you think?'

'So, what do you want me to do?'

'Well, I don't know exactly, Joe. I'd like the shoes to last a long time. I don't know what treatments are best. What will make them last longer?'

'I could put new heels on. I could add soles. I could spray the leather. What do you want?'

'I want the shoes to last, Joe. What do you recommend I do?'

'That's your choice. You tell me what you want me to do and I'll do it. I'm just a cobbler.'

Joe was not 'just a cobbler'. He was an expert in shoes and I was asking him to share his expertise to help me make a good decision about my shoes. I'm sure I had a budgetary limit, but

I'd have largely taken Joe's advice, whatever the cost, because he'd done a good job on previous pairs.

Think about your buying decisions. Isn't it wonderful when a salesperson knows all about a certain product or service and you can ask their advice about what to buy? You know they won't tell you to buy something unless it's right for you. And you know that they understand what you want. You can feel confident buying something based on their recommendation. That's what I mean when I say that we love being sold to. It's when we're helped and reassured by someone with knowledge, understanding and whom we trust. And we are thankful to that person when they enable us to make a good decision.

Now to our third myth, which for so long turned me away from sales as a career.

Shattering Sales Myth 3: sales is a rubbish job with no career prospects.
'Is there a more important function in business than sales?' asks Philip Delves Broughton in his book *Life's A Pitch,* a brilliant examination of the importance of sales in daily life. Philip is right, yet the importance of sales is constantly overlooked by people dismissing it as a serious career option.

For almost any job role, sales skills are imperative. For some of the best business roles available, a background in sales is the best breeding ground for a successful business future.

Where did Alan Sugar start the career that saw him build his company, Amstrad, from nothing to a market valuation at its peak of £170 million? What about James Caan, who also built his companies – Alexander Mann and Humana International –

into multi-million-pound operations before selling them for about £170 million? Lara Morgan built Pacific Direct, the beauty supplies company, from scratch to £20 million before selling it. Yes, they spent their early years honing their future business minds through the art of sales. Through the art of finding then engaging an audience in relevant, compelling conversations that moved that audience to give them money in return for their products and services. That's sales, and that, my friends, is business.

Asked in a *Sunday Times* interview about whether she'd ever been hard up, Lara Morgan said, 'Yes. When I took my first job which was in sales. If I didn't make sales, I didn't make any money. Thankfully I did. I would recommend a job in sales to anybody as a brilliant first job for a career in business.'

In 2012, aged thirty-seven, Sara Blakely became the then world's youngest self-made female billionaire. Sara is the founder of Spanx and her first job was selling fax machines door-to-door to businesses in New York. She found that her feet became hot and uncomfortable while she was walking and wondered why no company had yet created tights without feet. Spanx's first product was just that.

There are many stories from across the globe of successful business people who have learnt their trade through doing a sales job. Fifteen of them were interviewed for this book, and you can read their profiles as you progress.

Sales is not a rubbish job with no career prospects, but rather the foundation of all business and, therefore, one of the best places to start a business career.

When you understand sales, it's easy to see why successful people often start here. Sales is about finding a potential audience for a product or service you offer. Once you identify that audience, get what you do in front of them and understand each individual's needs to see if they're a good match for what you offer. If they are, give them clear and compelling reasons to take money out of their pockets, then ensure you deliver value and that they're happy with your product/service. At a later date, you can return to offer them even more value with a new product or service.

Business cannot exist without a successful sales function. In fact, I'd go as far as to say that society itself cannot function properly without sales. It's a bold statement, so allow me to explain briefly.

For most of us, taxes fund the basic needs of society: education, roads, health, police, etc. Taxes are charged for the most part on money changing hands (income tax on companies paying staff; VAT on buying things; corporation tax on companies that have generated profits based on clients paying them money; etc.). If sales are not made, if business is not done, then tax is not due. Without the critical function of sales, we could not pay for schools, hospitals, police forces or roads.

These damaging sales myths convince too many people that sales is not for them. It is truly a scandal that sales is so appallingly mis-sold. It's also ironic, of course. A job in sales is a great place to start your career and, in the next chapter, I'll give you ten reasons why you should at least consider it.

BUSINESS LEADER PROFILE

Lara Morgan

'Working in sales is an honour.'

From borrowing a suit from a friend for her first client pitch to selling her company for £20 million, Lara has an incredible story. Yes, it's founded on grit, hard work, business savvy and a healthy dollop of charisma, but it's also based on an experience of sales early in life.

Aged eighteen, Lara took her first steps into sales. Having seen her father's company go bankrupt, she had to provide for herself.

'I sold myself out of being poor and would recommend it as a career to anyone.

'I had no sales training whatsoever. I was completely ignorant. As far as I was concerned, I was just going out and having a conversation. Because I was oblivious of what I should be saying, I kept my mouth shut and people told me what they needed.'

The secret of so much sales success: listening rather than talking.

At twenty-three, Lara left her sales job and set up her own business, Pacific Direct, providing luxury toiletries into the hotel and hospitality industry. That's not to say that she stopped selling when she left a role with 'sales' in the job title, though.

'I'm still learning sales now. I still make mistakes. Each mistake gives you the opportunity to learn and not make that mistake again.'

Lara believes young people are missing out on an amazing place to learn business and she'd love to see more people consider sales as a career. Part of the problem, she believes, is that people leave the British education system knowing nothing about it.

'Sales should be on the curriculum along with finance and marketing. It's a no brainer.'

Contrary to the commonly held stereotypes surrounding sales, Lara remembers her first impressions.

'I quickly learnt that sales is actually about understanding somebody's problem and presenting a solution to take that pain away. It's common sense.

'But most people have challenging experiences of sales that leave them feeling manipulated. The public perception of sales is what you see. Car dealers. Estate agents. You don't see the attractive side of selling. Done properly, it's about a professional exchange of ideas and challenges.'

'If you can effectively meet the challenges sales conversations present, you are accelerated into a position where you can earn more money than you would in any other profession in the world. There is no ceiling on your earnings. You could earn more than your boss and that's a good thing.'

On the flipside, you can't just swan in on day one and walk away at 6pm with £1 million in the bank.

'Sales offers the opportunity to earn incredible amounts of money but you need to work very, very hard to earn it.'

To be successful in sales, it's important to be able to keep going when things get tough, as they inevitably will. As a leading triathlete, Lara draws a comparison with the sporting world.

'Good sportspeople and salespeople have get up and go. They'll fail and they get back up because they're so hungry to win. That resilience is essential.'

As well as hunger and resilience, what else does Lara look for in salespeople?

'People that understand the value of money and the hard graft required to earn it. If you have two people who are equally smart doing the exact same job, it's the one that puts in the most hours and is most persistent that will be more successful and earn more money. It's

down to you the amount of effort you put in and what you get out – see your name at the bottom of the sales leader board? Do something about it.'

Ultimately, sales takes a lot of hard work and determination. If you're able to bring that in abundance every day, you'll earn not only a great deal of money, but freedom of choice.

'Working in sales is an honour. If I wanted to retire at forty, I could. That choice is such a privilege.'

CHAPTER 2

The Hidden Career – Ten Reasons To Find It

'Job titles don't matter. Everyone is in sales. It's the only way we stay in business.'
HARVEY MACKAY

In my years of ignorance (and poverty), I wasn't aware of one good reason to go into sales. Every view I had was negative.

How wrong I was. There are many great reasons to go into sales, but I've limited the list here to the top ten.

Availability. There are sales jobs aplenty.

I have enormous respect for people who set themselves the goal of getting an exclusive job: a job that only ten people each year might get. Don't let me stop you aiming for that – I encourage you to go for it, but also give yourself other options.

First and foremost, you need to work. Working allows you to make money, and money helps you have choices in life. I cannot (yet) say I've been rich, but I have been pretty poor. Having money doesn't solve every ill of the world, but it's infinitely preferable to having no money or little money. So, give yourself choices by working.

Going to work gets you out of bed and makes you busy doing something productive, which has positive knock-on effects to the rest of your life. I have had times in my life when I didn't work, and I know in hindsight that they were bad times for me as a person. No matter what the work, any job is better than not working. So why not look for a job where there are plenty of vacancies?

There is a wide choice of sales jobs with real prospects, opportunities to shine and chances to develop a professional, successful, enjoyable career. Businesses are crying out for people who can build a sales career with them. You might not yet be feeling their love and desperate need to find you, but I assure you they're there.

Meritocracy. A job in sales can be harsh, let me not blind you to that. The world of business in its entirety can be harsh. However, sales has to be one of the fairest of professions. Truly. If you and I work for the same company doing the same sales job with the same resources and you do it much better than me, then you get paid more than me. Quite right too.

I do a lot of sales training with my company's clients. Before that, I worked in many different environments from small companies to large corporate beasts. Often, I have witnessed job dissatisfaction due to 'people earning the same or more money while not being as good as others at the job'. As human beings, we have an innate aversion to a lack of fairness. It kills motivation and, to a large extent, happiness.

Those working in sales teams will never enjoy being bottom of the sales league table, but it is difficult for them to complain about unfairness. Sales figures over a consistent period of time never lie. If you sell more than me most months, most years, then you are more successful than I am and will be paid significantly more. My failure would bother me, but it would be within my reach to change that.

The best people get the best rewards. That's meritocracy.

Variety. Sales is obviously not the only job that has variety, but it's one of the most varied. Even in the early weeks in the job, you'll be dealing with people, all sorts of them. Those people will have different needs, different ways of communicating and different preferences on how they make buying decisions. When you throw in the fluctuations in the economy, consumer confidence and seasonal buying habits, there is every likelihood that each day will be different, unpredictable and exciting.

Launch pad. The skills gained in a sales job are among the most transferable you can ever learn. Is there a job in which an ability to communicate well, understand an audience and offer compelling reasons to do business are not used? I doubt it.

Many people look at sales or marketing as first or second job options. I'd like to suggest choosing sales over marketing – it's a better launch pad.

In 2012, I gave a presentation on sales to 100 young entrepreneurs who were part of the *Shell Livewire Young Entrepreneur of the Year* awards in London. My interactive session lasted about an hour and introduced to them all the basics of how to construct successful sales conversations (we'll be covering this later in the book). Speaking before me was

Jennifer Layne Welch, Head of Brand Strategy and Stewardship at Shell. Her presentation on Shell and marketing was superb and a hard act to follow.

When I finished my hour on the sales essentials for entrepreneurs, she approached me with congratulations and her own story on the importance of sales skills in business, particularly in marketing. Soon after starting at Shell, she was told, 'You need to work with the sales team for a while – you're not understanding our customers yet.' She said that her six months in sales put her right in the firing line of customer-meets-product-and-tells-salesperson-what-they-think. It gave her an intimate insight into what makes customers say yes or no in a way that marketing never had. In short, her time in sales made her a better marketer.

Whether you have an eye on marketing or any other role in business, the lessons you'll learn in sales will equip you better to do that job.

Rare skill. The attributes, skills and habits required to be successful in sales are hard to find in one person. Much of my book will explain how simple sales theory is, but the execution of it day in, day out is hard. Just like running a marathon, you can understand what is needed remarkably easily, but it's difficult to do it.

Sales is tough. If you have the skills you need for sales and can prove you have them, you are quite a rare person, and that gives you bags of value in the marketplace. You will never be out of work for long, I assure you.

You must be confident, but not loud and boorish. You must be a good listener, but also be persuasive. Stay in touch with your clients enough to make them feel important, but not so much that they feel pestered. There are lots of lines that need to be drawn between one behaviour and another, and there are so many factors involved that there are rarely guidelines as simple as 'Always do x' or 'Never do y'. Add to that the fact that you must be hard-working, ethical, focused and well-organised (see Chapter 3 on The Ingredients For Success), and you can see why well-rounded sales skills are rare and much-prized.

Business essence. Sales is the very essence of all businesses, even those without a sales team. The words 'business' and 'sales' are practically interchangeable. All businesses need to:

1. Find an audience with a problem that needs solving
2. Develop a product or service that solves that problem
3. Find a way to get that product or service in front of the relevant audience
4. Take time to understand the audience's particular needs
5. Present the solution in a way that is compelling enough and clear enough to excite their audience
6. Deliver their solution in a manner that satisfies the audience by solving the problem, hopefully even more effectively than they expected
7. Stay in touch to ensure continued satisfaction and look for other problems to solve (then start the process all over again).

Now, in a larger company, your work in the sales team will not include every step of the process described above, but you will need to understand all the steps and interact with the people who deliver them (and the customers who are the recipients of each step). If any part of the seven-step process fails, then your ability to sell is affected whether you control that step or not. Make sure all steps are delivered well if at all possible.

Each conversation with product development, marketing, pre-sales team, after-sales team, customer service team, complaints department, finance and management builds your knowledge not just of how to do your sales job better, but about the world of business. Finally, as the contact person at the critical decision-making time with clients, you'll have the greatest insight into why people say yes or no. Understand that and you really do know business.

Uncapped earnings. In a sales role, your potential to earn is unlimited. If you are good, you can earn very good money. Here's a real-world example for you.

Gwen was twenty-four and, having graduated two years earlier, was working behind a bar in her home town. On an hourly rate, she was paid the minimum wage. One evening, a drunken customer sitting at the bar was being particularly difficult and Gwen's people skills kicked into life to save the situation from getting worse. She managed to persuade the tricky client to go home and the pub's friendly atmosphere was retained.

Also sitting at the bar – not being tricky – was the Managing Director of a local company with a sales team. *If she has the skills to handle people that well, she can probably sell,* he thought.

Two weeks later, Gwen started working for his company, and within three months had moved from an administrative role to the sales team. Three years later Gwen was the most successful salesperson in the company, and her salary plus commission and bonuses totalled £132,000 for the year. From minimum wage to £132,000 in just over three years – incredible.

What I find interesting about this is that the Gwen who made a six-figure income was the same Gwen who worked behind the bar for minimum wage. She had the same background, attitude and attributes. Yes, she had to be taught some sales skills, but that is relatively easy to do if all the other factors are in place.

In fact, she is the perfect example of the inspiration for this book: her ability to sell has benefitted her life, the company that employed her and the clients who bought from her. That ability could have remained undiscovered and unexplored but for the fact that she handled a tricky pub client well when a well-connected punter was sitting at the bar.

People around the world right now could be earning tens of thousands of pounds more than they are each year if they'd chosen a sales job.

Robust. Although I came to sales late in life, I have sold in both buoyant markets and struggling ones. Whatever the state of the wider economy, there is always work for successful salespeople. In fact, good salespeople are in higher demand, and therefore worth more money, when times are hard than when times are plenty.

When a market is on fire, almost anyone can make sales. Don't misunderstand me – make the most of those times and sell, sell, sell, but you'll really understand the robustness of your sales skills when a market starts to shrink.

Gerry Larkin – one of my favourite people in the world of property – is a wonderful example. From 1998 to 2005, Gerry was a successful media salesperson in the international property world. He was liked and trusted by all. Unfortunately for Gerry, soon after he set up his own property media company, the credit crunch of 2007/2008 finished off his young business. Even his good name in the market was unable to generate the cash he required to be successful.

He returned to his former employer to offer his services back to them. They'd have loved to have had Gerry on their team again, but the market was so bad, they simply had no funds to offer him his old job back. The robustness of his sales skills now kicked in.

He said to his old employer, 'I recognise the problem you face. I know how hard the market has become, believe me. What about this idea? I can work from home. I have my own phone line and my own computer. You do not need to pay me a salary, but you agree to pay me commission on any sales revenue I generate. You only incur costs if I make you money and you'll always be in profit on my work.'

His old boss could not refuse. Six months later, Gerry had generated more revenue than anybody else on the sales team. He was offered a job on an employed basis with a salary, plus, of course, the commission due on his revenue. He remains, five years later, the most successful salesperson at the company.

Gerry's sales skills kept him earning money even when no employer was able to employ him.

Good fun. Two or three years into my sales career, I was walking to work one morning and overtook a young couple. I was walking quite quickly and it must have been obvious that I was keen to get to work.

'Look at him,' I heard the young guy say. 'How sad. I hope I never want to get to work that quickly!'

His companion laughed in agreement.

'Forgive me for barging into your conversation,' was my reply. 'You are walking as slowly as possible to waste eight hours of your life doing a job you clearly hate. When you add a probable one-hour journey each way moaning about going to work or about having been at work, that's nearly a third of your life being unhappy. And I'm the sad one?'

When I say this was my reply, it was only in my head as I continued my speedy walk to work.

Even if you're not thinking about sales as a job, please don't accept the prevailing mood that work is some sort of sentence you have to serve in return for the freedom to have a few quid to stay alive. Work doesn't have to be your whole life, but it's a big part of your life so why not do it with passion, energy and a sense of fun?

In sales, providing you're the right sort of person for it, you'll work in a dynamic environment. Of course, not every minute will be fun, but within the context of what work is, it will be enjoyable. If you've never worked in a job that allows you to go home thinking, *Wow, that was a tough day and I know I did really well in spite of that difficulty*, then you're missing out on one of life's great feelings. You'll be both tired and energised. You'll enjoy your evening far more with a good day's work behind you, and you'll probably sleep better too. Try it. Then tell me if I'm wrong.

Good people. Much of your happiness at work is linked to the people with whom you spend your time. I'm not suggesting that you should only work with your best mates, but to be happy, you'll probably want to be among people you like, respect, and who inspire you. If nobody in your job inspires you, that's a problem – look elsewhere quickly!

Good salespeople are fun to be around. They usually have a good sense of humour (some would argue this is an essential skill), and an energy and focus that you can feed off. Trust me, if you're surrounded by downbeat people who moan all the time, you will likely become a downbeat person who moans all the time. All attitudes are contagious, and I believe that negative attitudes are the number one killer of choice for those seeking success in both business and life. They can seem inoffensive enough – 'My train was late today. Again. Then I couldn't get a seat. Of course… ' – but the moaning will slowly drive you mad.

A negative attitude, though, is more of a habit than an attribute. Habits are not easy to change, but it's possible. Firstly, recognise if you've become negative. Secondly, want to change that. Then, learn how to do that. There are far better people to help you do this than me. Try *The Power of Habit* by Charles Duhigg as a great book to get you started.

In sales, you need to be intelligent, tenacious, enthusiastic, well-organised, optimistic, flexible, mentally dextrous and healthy, physically and mentally. Surrounded by others like that, I find sales a top place to be.

I turned my nose up at sales for years and it was a massive mistake. Don't suffer from the same ignorance as I did. Make informed choices. If you now think it's worth considering, whether as a job, as a career skill for other jobs or to help you get on better with people in your personal life, let's look at what you need to be successful.

BUSINESS LEADER PROFILE

Chris Brindley

From stamping chequebooks to MD

Chris Brindley, MD of Metro Bank, really shouldn't have had the career success he's had. According to most accepted wisdoms, that is.

Raised by a single mother on a council estate in Manchester, he left school with very few qualifications. So how has he ended up as Managing Director of the newest and fastest growing bank in the UK, one that's revolutionising the sector?

During his interview with Metro Bank, Chris was told, 'You get the fact that the customer comes first. We want you to run our bank, but a bank without sales targets.' Let's go back in time a little to find out how this poorly qualified eighteen-year-old scaled the heights of the financial world before recreating it in his current role.

Chris's first job was stamping chequebooks at NatWest, a role he performed for a year. That started the finance route, but it was hardly a sales role.

'Early on, one of the managers highlighted three attributes he'd noticed in my work: I could get on with anybody; I was good at finding connections with people; and I had bags of energy. After a year of stamping chequebooks, I moved into HR to help find, train and retain talent at NatWest.'

The year 1989 saw a shift in the banking world and banks were able to provide third party mortgages. This was also a key shift for Chris as he became an Assistant Manager whose role was to sell these mortgages. His attributes were about to come in handy.

Chris's approach and execution, plus the success he brought, overcame the initial fears of colleagues and clients alike who had voiced concerns at him 'just being a salesman'. It started, as ever, with the right attitude.

'To me, you must start with the customer in mind, and therefore the first question should be "What does my customer really want?" She doesn't want a mortgage – why would she? She wants a home.

'Once you understand the customer, it's your job to delight them with the service you provide. I was a service provider at NatWest, and before I could provide that service, I had to build connection. People do business with those they like. We like people that show an interest

in us, that make us feel important and that deliver a service that meets and possibly exceeds our expectation.'

Chris's success is not exclusive to the world of finance. He also had a spell as National Sales Director at British Gas where he broke the record for boiler sales in a calendar month (in June would you believe?). It was the same starting point for Chris, whether he was selling boilers or mortgages.

'What does my client really want? Clients don't want a replacement boiler when theirs breaks down. That means several days without heating or hot water, probably in the middle of winter when they most need it. They want a really good quality boiler that gives value-for-money and doesn't break down. They buy quality and peace of mind, not price. But you have to take time to help them understand their needs and what they want.'

Chris is unequivocal about the most important ingredient in his career.

'My success has all been predicated on being able to understand people and provide them with the right products and services. I couldn't do what I do now without that, and I wouldn't even have this job, this life, without that skill and that experience. My job now is to stimulate thinking here at Metro Bank so that customers have the best possible experience.'

I suspect Chris stimulates thinking wherever he goes. I left my interview with him that day with both renewed inspiration and two practical changes to make in my working life. Firstly, that your working day starts the evening before by getting everything ready: clothes out, shoes polished, phone on charge, morning plans clear. It makes the morning more relaxed. Secondly, start the day with something motivational – a great example is to have some motivational speeches downloaded onto your phone. Kick the day off well and it's much more likely you'll have a good one.

Chris's story is an inspiration to every young person in the UK looking for their first or second job and wondering where it might all lead. He's got there from humble beginnings through hard work, focus and outstanding sales skills. What's stopping any of us from doing the same?

CHAPTER 3

The Ingredients For Success

'How you think when you lose determines
how long it will be until you win.'
GILBERT K. CHESTERTON

Contrary to accepted wisdom, I believe that anyone can be good at selling. This is partly due to the fact that there are many different ways to sell, and partly because most of the elements required for success are skills and habits. Both of these can be learnt.

I have spent several years teaching people how to sell. I have taught engineers, roofers, scientists, social workers and many more. None of them were doing sales as their primary job, but they had to sell within what they did (what Dan Pink calls 'non-sales selling' in his brilliant book, *To Sell is Human*), and I was able to help them do it better.

Does this mean that they all became brilliant salespeople? No, I'm sure they didn't – not because they couldn't, but because they didn't want to. Whether you want to learn these skills and put them into practice every day is an entirely different matter from whether you can.

In the following pages, I will introduce the elements so regularly found in salespeople that I think it reasonable to call them the 'ingredients of successful salespeople'. It's unlikely that any single salesperson is perfect at every one, but each successful salesperson will have learnt and developed a good number of them. If you recognise these in yourself or, importantly, have the desire to learn them, you should succeed at selling. Even if you're not going to enter sales as a career, these attributes will make you a better communicator in any field whatsoever.

Success attribute 1: curiosity. As this book is all about confounding popular (mistaken) wisdoms, let's kick off with what is all too often overlooked as a sales skill: the art of listening. I said in the first chapter that selling, done properly, is helping people make good buying decisions. You cannot do that unless you have a good understanding of not just the immediate need of the client (e.g. 'I want to buy this phone') but also of their life and how the product will fit into that. This is not easy, of course – 'I'd like to buy this phone, please,' says client. 'Mmm, before I can help you, tell me about your life' – but you'll read later how to do this effectively without driving an impatient client mad.

'I'm not a good listener' is one of my least favourite phrases in life. People suggest they were born with an inability to concentrate when other people are talking. This is ludicrous. Whether you listen to someone or not is 100% your choice in every instance – it's amazing how often those bad listeners hear something that is beneficial to them! We select when we listen and what we listen to.

There are times when we deliberately tune out of the concentration required to listen. By the time we're adults, this may have become a habit. In addition – and this is an important addition – we too rarely see any personal value in listening to what other people say. Our own stories are far more interesting to us, and told better.

To improve your skill as a listener, realise that listening to others will be hugely beneficial to you in life. In few working worlds is this truer than in sales, but it will help you in every job in every sector, and it will also help in your personal relationships. In sales, every piece of information that you need to help your prospective clients make good buying decisions is in the words they say, not the words you say.

But there's an even more important reason for listening well.

How does it make you feel when someone listens to you? I mean, *really* listens. I often find that it's easier to think of how you feel when people don't listen. Here's an example from my life.

In 2012, I was in a pub in Derby, having a drink with a few friends and family. I'd just spent the day delivering a session of my company's sales programme to undergraduates in Derby and Nottingham. The idea for this book came from the programme, which helps people understand both the benefits of sales as a career and a life skill no matter what job they do. The following morning, I was due to be interviewed about the programme on BBC Radio. It was quite a coup for me to have this level of media interest. (If interested, you can hear the interview in full via a link on my company's website: www.salestalentuk.com.)

While I was buying drinks at the bar, my brother told the assembled group about the media interview. As I returned, one friend said, 'So, Paul, I hear you're on BBC Radio tomorrow morning?'

'I am, yes.'

What happened next? Did the friend ask why I was on? What the interview was about? How I'd managed to get the coverage? All perfectly reasonable expectations, but wrong.

His next words were, in fact, 'I was interviewed myself by BBC Radio Derby many years ago.' He proceeded to tell the story of the interview, what the presenter asked him, why he was there, one or two funny things he'd said.

Another friend piped up next. 'Funny you say that, I was interviewed by BBC Radio Leicester in 1980.' And yes, the group all heard about that interview too. What did nobody around that table do?

Nobody said, 'Why are you being interviewed, Paul?' They didn't want to listen to me; they wanted to talk about themselves.

I witness conversations like this every day of my life. Not listening is the norm; to do well in sales, you need to break that. To realise how common this is, and recognise how frustrating it is, observe the conversations you have day-to-day with friends and family. Proper two-way conversations in which people really listen to each other are quite rare. What usually happens is that two or more people are in the same place at the same time, giving a series of monologues.

For example, you say, 'We've just booked our summer holiday to Italy.'

Your friend then replies, 'We went to Italy last year. It was amazing. We did this, saw that… etc.'

Or, you say, 'I need to get a haircut.'

Your friend replies, 'I just had mine cut, do you like it?'

Watch out for conversations like these. When I first noticed them, it ruined my social life for quite a while as I realised that nobody cared enough to listen.

So back to the question, 'How do you feel when people listen?' Well, when they don't listen, you likely feel that they don't care about you because they just want to talk about themselves. But when they do listen, you feel the opposite. They care about you, which makes you feel good. And that is the single biggest change you can effect in human communication as a whole, not just in sales.

To understand the impact of this change fully, see Chapter 7.

Great salespeople make people feel good about themselves by showing they care. They do this by listening, being genuinely curious and wanting to find out more. And it's a skill you can learn.

Success attribute 2: resilience. No matter how good you are at selling, you will always experience more failure than success. More people will say 'No thanks' than 'Yes please'. If you do not have the strength to overcome the feeling of rejection, then you are unlikely to be successful in a sales job. Resilience is a great asset, no matter what you do in life.

Without wishing to soften the harsh reality of rejection, I think people often fail to recognise how resilient they have already been throughout their life. Competitive people, for example, tend to be resilient. Whether you are competitive in a sporting sense or an academic one, or in any number of other pursuits, you push yourself to be challenged and, therefore, experience failure. Even stepping into a competitive situation, you're already showing bravery and the willingness to face failure. And after failing, you go back and try again. And in some cases, again and again and again. With each time you go back, you are being resilient.

This capacity to overcome failure – and by 'overcome', I mean accept it and try even harder to avoid it next time – is one of the most crucial elements in the success of any person in any walk of life. I often hear people talk about the difficulties of dealing with success. Honestly, success is relatively easy to handle. Failure is hard. Your ability to fail, try again, fail, try again and repeat has arguably shaped the person you are or will become. Do it well and you will, I promise, succeed.

As Winston Churchill famously said, 'Success is the ability to go from one failure to another without the loss of enthusiasm.' He could have been writing about successful salespeople.

Success attribute 3: confidence. If you're not the person who's the loudest in your group of friends, don't confuse that with a lack of confidence. Confidence is not about being the storyteller or joker, or the person who makes fun of other people and oozes self-importance.

Some of the best salespeople are not loud people who always want to be the centre of attention. A simple definition of confidence is 'A feeling of trust and firm belief in yourself or others', and you can learn confidence as you learn competence. When you're taught how to do something and have the chance to practise it repeatedly, you see improvements and get better results. You then start to believe in yourself more and become confident.

Learning how to drive is a great example. When I first started, I had no confidence in what I was doing at all. It was quite frightening and I could not believe that it was possible to control three pedals with two feet while steering, watching the road, being aware of other drivers' movements and navigating my way through unknown roads, never mind indicating, checking mirrors and chatting to my fellow passengers as I did all that. I lacked any confidence because I was incompetent.

Once I'd passed my driving test and had been driving for a few months, I was 100% confident in my ability to drive safely. I had learnt to be confident because I had become competent.

You can do the same with sales.

Of course, there are some people who seem 'born to sell'. Their friends will say they have the 'gift of the gab' and could 'sell anything to anyone'. In my work over the years recruiting and training salespeople, I have found two things. Firstly, very few such people exist; secondly, even fewer are good at sales as their 'gift of the gab' actually means they like the sound of their own voices too much to pay attention to their clients' needs. There are exceptions, just not many of them.

Typically, the people who seem to match sales have relatively well developed social skills by the time they start looking for work. They'll greet people warmly and confidently, probably because they've learnt from an expert how to do it well. It should really be taught in schools, but isn't. They'll feel comfortable in unfamiliar surroundings and with new people, plus they'll recognise that paying attention to the people they're with is the right way to behave in company.

If this sounds like you, you have a head-start in sales. If this doesn't sound like you, fear not – you can learn these things.

Success attribute 4: enthusiasm. The world is a better place when you're surrounded by enthusiastic people. I saw a lovely quotation on an office wall once, 'Attitudes are contagious. Is yours worth catching?', that reminded me that not only does a positive, enthusiastic outlook help in sales, it helps in all walks of life.

Salespeople make things happen. Whether it's a charity event, sporting fixture, community initiative or family occasion, they take an idea and work with it. I think such people have an abundance of energy and a positive outlook – making things happen takes an optimist in most cases. An optimist believes that everything will turn out well and then puts in the work to make that come true.

Success attribute 5: hunger. I started this list of attributes with the least expected for salespeople – curiosity – and I'm ending it with, arguably, the most important – hunger. Without hunger, the others become irrelevant.

Your hunger to succeed ultimately drives you forward as a salesperson. It makes you carry on when you have tough days. It keeps your enthusiasm topped up when it might start to flag on long, tired days at the end of long, hard weeks. It reminds you of the importance of your skills (they'll provide your successful future) and bolsters any bits of wavering confidence (nobody is 100% confident all the time). And it will force you to listen to your clients because if you want to achieve your goals, you need to understand them first.

Hunger, and the motivation it provides, can take many forms. For some, it's simple: they want to earn the money to afford a certain kind of life. Others want to be successful and the pursuit of excellence is what drives them. Some people want to prove others wrong – shame though it is that people are told, 'You can't do that', it can provide a real incentive to show that they can. See the story of millionaire businesswoman Caroline Marshall-Roberts, the business leader profile in Chapter 5.

Finally, some people are desperate. I was. At thirty-two years of age, I was completely broke and alienated from my friends as they could eat, drink and holiday in places I could never afford. And I made a resolution: 'This is not going to be my life. I will do whatever it takes to change it.' There was no doubt that hunger kept me going when things got tough. Now my hunger to give you the chance to avoid the mistakes I made is what fuels these words I am writing.

There are other attributes that will help you in a sales job, or any job that involves an element of selling, but these five are at the heart of most successful salespeople across the world: curiosity, resilience, confidence, enthusiasm and hunger. As you read that list, you may be working out which ones you have, but beware! You're often the worst person to judge. Read on and you may see that you match the above list more than you realise.

BUSINESS LEADER PROFILE

Mike Tobin OBE

Engineer to CEO and a swim with sharks

An engineering apprentice at the age of twenty, Mike Tobin was to become CEO of the leading data centre business in Europe, Telecity, a company he took from a market cap of £6m to almost £3bn in a little over a decade. Such an amazing story clearly had many twists and turns, many decisions that shaped an incredible life, but arguably the first one in his business life was born out of boredom.

'As an engineer for a computer company, my job was to fix computers that went wrong after we'd sold them. The trouble was nobody was selling any computers so I didn't have much to do! I picked up the Yellow Pages and looked for companies that might be interested in

what we were doing and then I called them. I got lucky on my first call and made a sale.'

The engineer became a salesman, and the salesman became one of the UK's most successful (and least conventional) CEOs.

'I quickly learnt that you have to sell yourself first. You must build trust with your potential clients. If you abuse that trust, you quickly lose the customer.'

After beginning his sales career unintentionally at twenty, he was MD of the French computer company, Goupil, by twenty-two.

'Sales is about understanding people's needs. If you do that well, that's what you need in management too. I had the technical knowledge from my apprenticeship and I quickly picked up the sales skills. So, at a very young age, I was actually well-equipped for senior management roles which was not necessarily what I'd expected when leaving school at sixteen.'

Mike's was a stratospheric and speedy rise up the corporate ladder with only a short time in a direct sales job. However, the lessons he learnt played a key part in his ability to grow companies and build teams in what has been an outstandingly successful career.

'I had a mentor early on, Ian Watson, who taught me key lessons. First, learn to say no in sales. If you say yes to everything, strong buyers will drive you down on price much too easily.

'Second, never take a client's no as a negative thing. It's a step closer to getting a yes. See it as an opportunity. Ask questions to understand

why they said no. Learning that lesson has shaped my career more than any other. Imagine the salesperson who thought that every call would be a deal. If you're afraid of failure, you won't make the calls. If you recognise that every failure is a step closer to a win, you'll do it more. If you don't have the mentality to handle that in order to earn more money and change your life, then you probably won't do sales well.'

What would have happened to Mike's career if people at his first company had been successfully selling computers so that he could have fixed them?

'We'll never know that answer, I guess. But I do believe that my ignorance of sales at that age should be addressed but, thirty years later, we still don't teach people about this key skill and the advantages it offers.

'We should empower kids to learn how to sell. Teach them to respect themselves, believe in themselves. If they learn to sell themselves, they'll be much better prepared. When selling yourself, think of yourself as a product. Why would someone want to buy you? Once you think about that and can present that, you have a much better chance of getting any job, not just one in sales.'

No article about Mike Tobin and his career can fail to mention his unconventional take on management and, in particular, motivation. He is renowned for taking his teams out of their comfort zones.

When merging Telecity and Redbus in 2006, Mike saw that the management team was worried about the impending changes. Did he sit them down to reassure them? No, he took them to

Scotland where they donned wetsuits to swim with sharks. There were no cages to protect them.

'They were terrified before getting into the water. Once in the water, they were still terrified though also excited. I asked how they felt afterwards and they said they were so happy they did it. I asked them to remember this in future – when you face something frightening, it's rarely as bad as one fears. You'll survive and you'll learn.'

Maybe an early experience in Bond St Station, when he was reading the offer letter for his engineering apprenticeship, influenced Mike more than even he realises. A man spotted him and, having half read the letter over Mike's shoulder, gave him a tip: 'Always go the extra mile, young man. There's less traffic there.' The evidence since then suggests it was a good tip that Mike has followed in many different ways.

CHAPTER 4

The Secret Skill – Four Simple Steps

'Everything should be made as simple as possible, but not simpler.'
ALBERT EINSTEIN

'I'm not really a salesperson,' people tell me all the time. Yes, you are. You just don't call it selling.

'I don't have the gift of the gab and you need that in sales,' others say. No, you don't.

Another widely held belief is 'You can either sell or you can't – it's not something you can learn.' Yes, you can.

We all sell every day, whether it's to ourselves ('Should I go for a run this morning or not?'), selling an activity to our family or friends ('I really want to go to the Arsenal match/swimming pool/adventure park'), or asking for more spending money from parents, lower rent from landlords or entry to a concert in the VIP area. In all of those examples and thousands more, we are trying to convince an audience to do something in the way we want them to do it. Any communication that seeks to change what people think, do, know or feel falls under the discipline of sales.

To teach you the basics of sales, I use the business world as the starting point. Once you know how to sell in a work context, that can be translated into the personal world.

Do you remember the exercise I mentioned earlier where I ask people to sell to their friend? I used that example to show you that sales does not mean talking all the time, which is always harder than people think it will be. After a slightly awkward start in the exercise, people generally describe their product in glowing terms.

'This coat is not just warm – among the warmest available – but it is also stylish. Look at how it hugs your body shape well. You look amazing. The pockets are lined which gives added comfort…etc. etc.'

They list a range of features as they come to mind (pockets, hood, lining, easy-to-wash), but after around thirty seconds, they run out of new content and start repeating things.

'Yes, so… it's really warm. And you can see the style. It's really stylish… '

By forty-five seconds, they've completely run out of things to say and probably try to get their friend to buy before the minute is up. For most people, it feels like a long sixty seconds.

I'm going to show you a way to sell that's easier and better, for your future clients as well as for you. But before I do that, let's think about the customer for a moment.

I normally ask the attendees at my courses to imagine what their attempted sales conversation would have been like for a real customer. How would a potential customer have felt after a minute of hearing why a coat/pen/phone is the best for them? Would they have felt pressured? Uncomfortable?

Probably both. That's how most of us feel when we're sold to by someone talking at us, and this is why so many people think of salespeople as pushy. We don't want to feel that way, so we don't buy from that person, even if they're selling something we want. More importantly, this impression of sales makes us feel that we don't want to do sales ourselves because we'd be making people feel uncomfortable every day. That would be awful, wouldn't it?

But it's not true. If you sell properly to people, then you won't make them feel uncomfortable. As I mentioned earlier, selling done properly is about helping people make good buying decisions. Talking at people doesn't help any customer make a good buying decision, because the salesperson won't know what sort of coat/pen/phone they like. This leads to a blind pitch of a product based on assumptions about the customer, not based on what they actually want. Different people will buy the same product as others but for different reasons. Unless salespeople take time to understand each customer's reasons, they'll be limited in the success they'll enjoy.

Let's examine how to sell in the right way in a simple four-step structure that came to me in a moment of clarity. I was sitting in a hotel bar in Ireland a few years ago with only a pint of Guinness for company (sales training can be a lonely world), having spent the day training sixteen young sales executives for a global technology company. They were in the early weeks of their working lives and they'd just learnt one of their most important lessons. And so had I.

In their relatively short time in the job, they'd learnt so much information about their new market, their company's products and services and how to present them in a sales conversation that I thought we should put their knowledge to the test by asking them to make some calls to real clients. They were a little nervous but willing to give it a go.

The calls were disastrous. They stumbled through the conversations. Their questions were poor. When they did talk about their company and its services, they ran out of things to say after only thirty seconds or so.

When we came together again after an hour of calls, they were amazed that they'd had so little to say.

'What happened to all the information we'd learnt?' they cried.

Now, this was partly the point of putting them on the phones in the first place. They were, until then, under the impression that they knew all they needed to know. I wanted them to realise that they had content, yes, but that they did not yet know how to present that content when under the pressure of talking to a real person.

But the lesson I learnt was even more important. The training I was giving them was good, but it was too complicated. They needed to retain so much information in their brains that it was critical they had a structure to their conversations that was simple.

As I enjoyed my Guinness, reflecting on the day's events and the need for simplicity in sales, it became clear to me. My thoughts, not the Guinness. During my years of selling and delivering sales training, I'd had thousands of conversations myself and listened to thousands of other people's sales calls and meetings. That evening, I recognised the four steps they all went through, and those steps, in most cases, came in the same order. They're easy to follow and they're completely customer-friendly. And as you'll see, they are just common sense, really.

I'll introduce the four steps and how to use them shortly, but first I'd like to make a quick point to address any fears about the rigidity of using a set structure when dealing with different people. Didn't I say that we need to deal differently with every person and not make assumptions?

I always ask to speak to the people I'll be training before creating their training content. I talk to them about how they prepare for their sales conversations and whether they practise. A regular response from them is that they can't really prepare or practise because every client is different and this means that every conversation is different. In response, I ask them if they really believe that every conversation is completely different and they almost always say yes.

Then I ask them to record their phone calls to clients for one full day, and listen to those calls before we speak again. Once they have listened to the calls, I ask them the same question I asked before: 'Do you believe that every conversation is completely different?' The evidence is compelling that the conversations are actually quite similar, and they've now heard it themselves.

No client conversation is identical, of course, but the basic structure is largely the same. You'll ask similar questions and mention key selling points of your product or service. That means you can prepare and you can practise these, combining them with flexibility to change tack if and when you need to. You cannot prepare for everything, but that doesn't mean you should prepare for nothing. Flexibility alone will not be good enough.

Although the four simple steps to successful sales conversations mostly come in the same order, perversely I'm going to start at step three.

What is one step that you have to take in order to make a living as a salesperson? What's one thing you must do at some stage? By the way, all of the questions I'll ask you will have simple answers – don't over-think this!

You must… *sell.* No matter how consultative you are, no matter how long you take to understand your client, you don't make any money unless you succeed in selling something. However, that step – the step most think of when they first start selling – does not come until the penultimate stage of a sales conversation. So much else should come first.

The sales pitch with no information is difficult to deliver and unlikely to succeed in a sale. It will almost never result in a productive sale in which you have helped someone to make a good buying decision. We'll come back to how you sell shortly, but let's uncover the rest of the structure first. The third step is to sell. Let's work back from there.

If we agree that selling is the process of helping someone make a good buying decision, what should we do in our sales conversations before trying to sell something? We find out what they want to buy and why they want to buy it, and lots of other things too. How do we find this out? We ask the customer, of course.

Step two in a productive, consultative sales conversation is to *ask* questions. This is the most important part of any sales conversation and a brilliant skill for everyone, no matter what job they do. But let's stick with salespeople for now. Through asking questions, we learn about our client, understand what they're looking for, why they want it, how they want to buy it. This makes the sales step of our conversation far more tailored, far better informed and much more relevant for our prospective buyer. In effect, we are simply matching our products or services to the needs they have already expressed.

I've heard many salespeople who are trained to ask questions as the first step, but I don't believe this is the best way. A real call from my mobile phone supplier illustrated the potential problem with asking questions first. It went something like this:

Company: 'Hello, Paul. This is David from Company X. How are you today?'

Me: 'Fine, thanks.'

Company: 'That's great. How is your new phone working out for you?'

Me: 'Okay.'

Company: 'Excellent. I see you're on Talk Plan A – are you happy with that?'

Me: 'I haven't really looked at it, David, but I guess it's okay.'

Company: 'I see your average bill is £xx – is that the amount you were expecting?'

At this stage, I didn't answer David's question and instead asked a question of my own.

Me: 'Sorry, David, what's the point of this conversation for me?'

I forget David's exact answer, but it was something along the lines of, 'We just need an update on how our service is working for you.' I replied that there was no apparent benefit to me in that conversation, and he mentioned a survey of all clients. Again, how does that help me?

You may think that I'm an impatient old codger – a salesman who needs to be 'sold' quickly or I get grumpy. In fact, salespeople are brilliant customers to sell to; providing you do it properly, salespeople like being sold to and respond to it well. But, yes, we're perhaps a bit more demanding in the standard we expect. Why should we give the next two minutes of our life to the salesperson who is calling us? If they fail to answer that question at the beginning, we will be much less likely to speak to them, answer their questions and listen to what they have to say.

The first step of any sales conversation is, therefore, to *earn* the right to speak. Give your prospective customer a reason to speak to you today. If they see a benefit, they will answer your questions. As they answer, you will build an understanding of what they want and discover whether you can help. If you can, you have the chance to explain how your service or product will help them.

If you work in retail, you may be shaking your head about this starting point. I agree. You're right. When someone walks into your shop, they have already expressed an interest in what you are selling, seen your brand and at least a selection of your products in the shop window. You would therefore be well served by beginning with questions. For all other sales, though – phone-based or field-based – you must first earn the right to speak.

So we have our first three steps:

- **E - earn** the right to speak to your prospective client
- **A - ask** questions to understand their needs
- **S - sell** your product or service in a way that serves the needs they've expressed.

If we have got this far, what should we do at the end? At my interactive workshops, at this point people usually say, 'Close the deal!' and to some extent they're right. Often, though, you won't close the deal at this stage, but always close the *conversation*. You do that best – and by 'best', I mean it's best for you *and* for the buyer – by agreeing a simple next step. I call that step *yes or no*.

This is not a hard sell tactic, I assure you. The structure I recommend could not be further from a hard sell, but you are not being helpful to your buyer if you do not help them to decide upon a simple next step. That is done best through offering them another call, a meeting, a follow-up appointment of some sort with an agreed date and time. It could also be a deal to buy what you offer, of course, but that's not the only way to close a sales conversation.

So, the final step is:

- **Y – yes or no** to an agreed next step.

If you fail to earn the right to speak to your customer at the beginning of your call, the conversation ends anyway, so that must come first. You obviously need to agree a next step and that's going to be at the end. So only the ask step and the sell step can really move, and sometimes they do. There will be times when a client will want to know more about you and your company before they answer your questions properly, but the aim is always to move to the ask step as soon as possible. It's better for you and, importantly, gives a better experience to your prospective customer too.

So we have four EASY steps to successful sales, though I'm afraid doing them is much harder. Like so many things in life, the theory is simple but the execution is difficult. The EASY structure helps you to learn how to sell well, especially when you first start selling, but no structure can make the complex interaction that is sales easy. So over the next few chapters, I'll give you more detail on each of these four steps to help you understand the challenges and show you ways to overcome them.

BUSINESS LEADER PROFILE

Julie Rodilosso

The £12 million woman

Leaving school with few qualifications is often seen as the worst possible start to a successful career. Yet, having been brought up by her mother in South Africa, Julie Rodilosso went from such an inauspicious beginning to become one of the UK's most successful insurance entrepreneurs. She founded insurance services business Rarrigini & Rosso in 1995, building it from scratch to a multi-million pound company employing 200 people. In 2003, she sold the company for nearly £12 million.

Now Founder and CEO of The XS Cover Company, she continues to be at the forefront of innovative insurance solutions, driving the business forward to become her next success story.

'I am passionate about what I do and that's such an important part of success. It's not the only thing you need but it's a hell of a good start!'

Julie's choice of sales at the beginning of her career was mostly driven by a lack of options.

'The few qualifications I had didn't make me an obvious winner for potential employers. But I had the ability to get on well with people and the confidence to give things a go. I was comfortable talking to people, looking them in the eye and being straight with them. I didn't realise it then but those attributes made me perfect for sales.'

She was successful very quickly in what was to become a glittering career. What were the skills she learnt in sales that helped her to this success?

'First, you have to be honest with your clients. You need drive, hunger – without that, you have nothing (and that isn't just true with sales). You also need empathy – you must see the world from the client's point of view and help them to move forward with a decision. Finally, you have to get to know your product, your clients and your market. They want expert advice and you need to turn yourself into that expert.'

Like all successful people, Julie first had to learn how to deal with failure.

'Whenever I failed to sell to people, I asked myself, "What am I doing wrong?" In the early days, I wasn't handling objections well. Salespeople generally do this badly and I was no different. But I learnt quickly!'

For Julie, the learning process should never stop.

'I learn something every day, I really do. The day I stop doing that, I'm finished. In the early days, I learnt how to be ready for objections and find ways to overcome them. However, I also learnt that it's pointless to beg for new business. If you've taken time to understand a client and present a compelling solution to their problem but they're not ready, come back later.'

As in all fields, when you see results with your new skills and understanding, your confidence builds and that leads to more success.

'Confidence is great, but must be tempered with a bit of humility otherwise you become unbearable. That combination can be difficult to balance.'

What are Julie's tips for those early in their careers?

'If you have certain attributes then sales is a truly great job. Some of the best jobs in the world are in sales and some of the most successful people in business are from a sales background. Providing you learn the processes and get good training, you'll be amongst the highest paid people.'

And what are the attributes needed?

'Hunger always. Confidence with a sense of humility too. Empathy. Someone that has learnt or can learn processes and stick to them. People with a military background can make brilliant salespeople and I always like seeing that on a CV.'

During our interview, Julie's enthusiasm and vitality were palpable. She's an evangelist, passionate about the work she does and the help it gives her clients. I think all truly great salespeople have this belief in the work they do. Julie clearly knows how to connect to people and uses it to build credibility and, through that, trust. Her track record also proves that she knows how to create business processes that work and therefore scale.

She's also instantly likeable. Although the whole point of the interview was to talk about her career, she took time to ask questions and showed a genuine interest in my answers. I left feeling lucky to have spent two hours with her and inspired to achieve my goals with the passion she has brought to hers. That's how great salespeople and great leaders leave people feeling. And it's a magical thing to be able to do.

BUSINESS LEADER PROFILE

Chris Townsend OBE

London 2012 and £2 billion

Chris Townsend was awarded an OBE in 2013 for his services to the London 2012 Olympic Games. As Commercial Director, he had the responsibility of generating the funds required to host the games. Without the work he and his team did, London 2012 would probably not have been the resounding success it was.

Chris credits much of this success (along with many others he's achieved throughout his career to date) to the skills he developed during the first few years after graduation, working in sales. Chris first dabbled with sales during the summer holidays, buying cars, doing them up and selling them on.

'I could see it was a stepping stone. A great foundation for my career.'

After graduating in Geography and looking for a challenging role that fed his passion for music, Chris beat over 2,000 other applicants to a field sales role with EMI Records. Out of the twenty-one territories in the UK at the time, his new patch in the Midlands was the worst performing.

'Within four months, we were top of the sales league.'

It was to be the first success of many.

'People often hold misconceptions about what the sales process involves and how complex it is. There's more to selling than just selling. Selling is the art of negotiation and the process merely begins at the pitch.'

Even before the pitch, there's a mountain of work.

'When I moved from EMI to selling HP products into retail, it was a case of going through the Yellow Pages Directory and calling companies from there.'

This business sourcing work, often seen as a relatively junior task, should not be underestimated. Its importance was underlined when London 2012 was just getting started.

'I had a blank piece of paper and I had to find contacts to sponsor the Olympics. I called companies myself and then went with Seb Coe and Paul Deighton to over 100 meetings to sign just one sponsorship deal. It was the planning and persistence I learnt from sales that allowed me to do that.'

As with any job, sales has difficulties and it demands a lot from those who work in it.

'Nine times out of ten it's not very rewarding. It requires a huge amount of planning and persistence to get just one deal. But that one in ten win makes it completely worthwhile.'

Chris urges every young person searching for success in any area of the corporate world to spend time working in sales.

'It gives you an understanding of the customer, the concept of selling and how to make it work. You develop negotiation and people skills that are invaluable in both business and life. I know a lot of people that work in finance and marketing that don't have those skills because they haven't experienced the sales process first-hand.

'I have always retained the skills I learnt in sales and continue to use them now. Sales has taught me an awful lot about people, their behaviour, how they communicate and how to get a positive response. When I moved into marketing roles, those skills were critical.'

'If you do it well, the rewards can be outstanding, giving you lifestyle choices as well as transferable skills. You need to be able to handle the extent to which sales exposes your strengths and weaknesses and address them. You'll learn life skills quicker than you would in any other department which puts you in a great position for the future.

'Without the resilience and planning skills I learnt from sales, I would not have been able to generate the £2 billion needed to host the London 2012 Olympic Games.'

CHAPTER 5

Grab Me And Make It Quick

'We don't know where our first impressions come from or precisely what they mean, so we don't always appreciate their fragility.'
MALCOLM GLADWELL

First, three bits of good news: this first step is the shortest part of your conversation, it's the easiest part to prepare and it's the easiest to practise. Now the bad news: despite being the shortest, it's actually the hardest part to do when you first start selling.

There are many different environments in which you can sell: over the phone, face-to-face at a meeting or an event, in a shop, etc. I'm going to introduce you to the EASY sales structure using a sales conversation over the phone as the example. Why? It's probably the hardest way to sell, so if you learn how to do this well, you should find the other types relatively easy. Also, it's more likely your first sales role will be over the phone – most salespeople start in a telesales role, and there are lots of jobs available to get you started.

I'm going to add a further level of difficulty by making the call I use as the example a first call to a brand new client. Among the scariest things you can do in sales – in business, in fact – is calling people when they're not expecting to hear from you, and it is a real skill. Sorry, I should qualify that – calling people when they're not expecting to hear from you and *doing it well* is a real skill. Too many people do it badly, and that takes very little skill (though quite a lot of courage).

The first problem you're likely to face is fear of disturbing someone. This will annoy them and they'll take that out on you. That, in turn, will make you even more afraid of the next call.

This mindset will clearly kill your desire to sell, but remember, you're bound to be nervous doing something you haven't done before. Can you think of anything completely new that you tried out and found you were good at it immediately? If you're honest with yourself, I suspect the answer will be no. I can't help you to build your confidence by saying, 'Be confident!' You gain confidence from knowing how to do something and then practising it.

Forget your mindset for now. What are the skills required to start new business phone calls?

First, let's address the biggest problem. You want to engage in a conversation with a stranger who is not expecting to hear from you and is not thinking about the product/service/idea that you want to speak about. When they answer the phone and realise it's not a friend, lover or congratulations from the lottery fund, they are likely to think, *Oh no, a stranger wants to engage me in a conversation – how do I stop them?*

Many salespeople have been trained over the years to overcome this negative reaction by asking friendly, non-threatening questions such as 'How are you today?' or 'Are you enjoying the lovely sunshine?' This, so the belief runs, shows they care and are not just calling to sell something.

Really? A stranger asks me how I am and that makes me think they care about me? It's supposed to build rapport with people and make them more likely to speak. I disagree.

Think of my example in the last chapter. My mobile phone provider started the call by asking me questions that gave nothing of value to me and just made me ask why they were calling me. If they had added questions about my health, my travel to work, my happiness with the weather today, it would have become even more pointless. If I wanted to talk about how I'm feeling today, I'd probably call a friend.

You rarely build rapport by contacting strangers over the phone and engaging in small talk. You're just wasting their time.

If someone answers their phone, they are free to speak, and they now want to know if it's worth talking to you. It's time to tell them. That does not mean selling them something as quickly as possible, but it does mean giving them some proof of value.

It's probably already clear that I think structure is important in sales conversations. In fact, I think it's important in most conversations, particularly business ones. I don't like scripts, but I do like structures. They should always be simple and, if possible, kept to three steps.

Earning the right to speak comes in three steps and I'll deal with them separately before bringing them back together.

- Introduction
- Reason for call
- Question.

Earn the right: introduction. The person you're calling does not know who you are. They don't know where you're calling from, i.e. which company. And they probably don't know the link between you and them (if there is any). The first thing to do, therefore, is make your identity clear to them.

Let's use my mobile phone provider as our example and see if a better structure can help the salesperson, David, to get me talking.

David: 'Good morning, Mr Owen. This is David calling from MPP. You upgraded your mobile phone with us four weeks ago.'

Good start, David. No, he's not earned the right to speak to me yet, but within the first few seconds I know who he is and I recognise the trigger (my phone upgrade) that's led to the call.

Earn the right: reason. Your prospective client really does want to know the point of the conversation in order to make a decision about whether the call continues or not. It's time to give some framework to the call and, if suitable, a suggestion of the value you may be able to offer. Importantly, if you've done the introduction well, the customer is listening now.

Over to David.

'The specific reason for my call today, Mr Owen, is to understand how well the first few weeks of the upgrade have gone for you and, if relevant, to introduce a new function that could make your phone even better.'

Hurrah! I know what David wants. I know that there might be some benefit to me. Before I learn of that benefit, he needs to ask me some questions, which nicely sets the agenda for the call too.

What else did David say in this revised introduction?

'The reason for my call today' is a signpost. It tells me that the question I have in my head (possibly unconsciously) is about to be answered. We use signposting all the time in our day-to-day conversations.

'Did I tell you what my brother did last week? Oh, I must tell you, you'll love this… ' You're telling your friend to listen carefully with a signpost of the story's relevance to them. But too often we overlook signposting in business conversations, particularly sales conversations. It's a brilliant way to start business conversations over the phone, sales or not.

Adding the word 'specific' makes the reason sound more important, more considered. It's not just any old reason. So as a salesperson, find a specific reason to call. If you can't find one, why on earth are you calling?

A final point on David's new 'reason' is that he uses my name. You don't have to do this, but it works really well. 'There is no sweeter sound to any person's ear than the sound of their own name,' wrote Dale Carnegie, author of the global bestseller *How To Win Friends And Influence People*.

If you don't quite agree on the importance of names, remember how you feel when someone gets your name wrong. It can be slightly offensive, a little hurtful. I work very hard in the corporate training sessions I run to learn people's names as early in the day as possible and to use them often (not too often – that can sound insincere). I'm human so I make mistakes, and the look on people's faces when I get their name even slightly wrong (Louise instead of Louisa was one such mistake I made) tells me immediately that it matters, despite what they might say afterwards.

Back to our call opening. We've introduced ourselves, our company and the trigger for the call. We've given the customer a reason to speak, making clear some potential value.

Earn the right: question. Effectively, so far, David has said, 'This is me. This is a good reason to speak to me today.' The final step, a question, is there to say, 'Now it's your turn to speak.'

You may be thinking that this is all obvious. It is, but it's also important to keep things simple. There are many problems with winning people's attention at the start of a phone call. One of them is that you only have a small percentage of their attention. They're in their office looking at their computer screen, or at home making a cup of coffee, or dropping their kids at school, or buying some milk, or trying to find their car keys, or looking at a map on their phone as they're lost. Whatever it is they're doing, your challenge is to take them out of their world and into yours. That is difficult.

Sometimes it's impossible – don't worry about those times. If you're to have any chance at all of getting enough of their attention to have a meaningful conversation, they don't just need to hear what you say. They need to *digest* what you say. In order to respond properly, they must have digested the content of what you've said and how it relates to them. If they haven't done that, you're very unlikely to get more than a few seconds of their time.

When people are feeling a little disorientated – which might well be the case when you're calling them while they're busy – then it helps them to have clear, simple instructions on what to do next. What easy and direct question could David from the mobile phone provider have asked me? Let's put it all together and see.

'Good morning, Mr Owen. This is David calling from MPP. You upgraded your mobile phone with us four weeks ago. The specific reason for my call today, Mr Owen, is to understand how well the first few weeks of the upgrade have gone for you and, if relevant, to introduce a new function that could make your phone even better. So, are you happy with the phone so far?'

If David had introduced himself in this way, I would probably have spoken to him. He's made the effort to prepare himself to start the call well. He's made clear the link to him, the trigger for the call and the potential benefit. Finally, he's had the good grace to stop talking and give me the chance to speak.

That's a better use of my time and David's. It's also a far better use of the mobile phone provider's time, because the careless way David originally introduced himself resulted in an unproductive call to a loyal client. And the company tried to call me again nine times – what a waste!

When you are calling people for the first time to talk business, it is very important to start the conversation well. It makes no difference if you're calling someone who's a complete stranger or someone who has asked your company to call them. It remains for many people the hardest part of all sales conversations, yet I continue to be surprised how little training people are given to do it well.

If you don't do this part well, you rarely have the chance to ask your clients and prospective clients any questions. If you don't ask questions and hear their answers, there is no way for you to understand their needs. If you don't understand their needs, you can't sell them anything useful or relevant.

The three-part structure above is not the only way to open sales calls, but it's one of the best, and a great place for you to start if you decide to give sales a try. The content will change a little sometimes, but not that much. Once you feel confident with the words you're saying, then think about the way you say them. The impact you have when you first start talking to people is not only affected by the words you use, but also by your tone of voice.

Now you know the words and structure to use, how can you give yourself the best chance of matching those words with the right tone of voice?

BUSINESS LEADER PROFILE

Sion Davies

The motivational force of student debt

By the age of thirty-five, Sion Davies was responsible for the success of a £130m business which landed Microsoft as its first client and hasn't stopped growing since. Area Sq, the commercial property fit-out company for which he works, has enjoyed such success in recent years that Sion said, 'The recession didn't really happen for us.' Sounds great! But how did Sion get to this position?

Graduating with a degree in Physics (getting a third – 'I still kick myself for that. Though it's had no effect on my career whatsoever,' he says), Sion had never thought of a career in sales. While on the Enterprise Rent-A-Car management trainee scheme, he saw an advert in the paper for a job with on-target earnings of £180,000. This was a whole new level in comparison to the £14,000 he was being paid at the time and, out of desperation, he applied for it.

Sion's entrance into the challenging world of sales wouldn't have happened, he says, if he hadn't had £25,000 student debt.

'I was driven by fear of that debt. In my first sales job, I'd get the train at 5.30am so I could be in the office at 6.15am, hours before everyone else, because this is when the Finnish market opened for the day.'

It wasn't that debt alone that led to Sion's success, though; a lot of it was because he had the right mindset.

'After a while, it dawned on me that if I work hard, I can get anything I want. In sales, hard work pays off. You can't substitute that.'

It was a rewarding though tough start in sales. So tough that just six months down the line, he was the longest serving employee. Although it wasn't what Sion would consider the perfect job by any stretch of the imagination, it had a huge impact on his future.

'I was fortunate to be desperate – it made me take the job and experience a difficult environment that led me to where I am today. It taught me so much.'

Reflecting on his start, Sion notes that the skills he learnt in his first sales jobs are used to this day. The one that translates to management the most strongly is ownership.

'In a sales environment, if you don't meet your targets, the company won't meet theirs, and even if you aren't sacked, you'll be made

redundant. Sales is very honest, you can't hide. You have to own your results – it's up to you to make a difference each day. The thing that haunts me is someone not making a difference and that's something sales, by its very nature, allows you to do.'

Sion remains confused by the misconception surrounding sales.

'It's considered something that only people that can't do other jobs do and that's not true. Most of the top people in our sector started in sales and they've grown their companies from there.'

There is, unsurprisingly, no shortcut to a successful career in sales, but the rewards are massive.

'The rewards are whatever you want them to be. A huge number of successful leaders will have come from a sales background. It teaches you so much more about people and gives you vital skills you need to succeed in management, too.'

Along with many other leaders who started in sales, Sion is frustrated by the fact that anybody has the ability to get into sales, yet relatively few do.

'There's a British-ness about not going into sales. Salespeople aren't made, you have to learn how to do it. You can't replace the work ethic, but you can teach people how to present their ideas better. Once you learn how to do it well, you have so many options.

'If you're positive and hard-working, sales is the best way to start your career and succeed quickly. Sales gets you to where you want to be quicker than any other profession.'

BUSINESS LEADER PROFILE

Caroline Marshall-Roberts

Proving people wrong

The daughter of an academic and the younger sister of a highly academic brother, Caroline didn't really like school that much. She was perfectly capable, just not interested. When she left school at 16, her parents didn't appear to have particularly high expectations for her.

'I do not remember anyone saying "Well done" to me at any time during my childhood.'

Aged eighteen and lacking confidence in her ability to do anything of merit, she didn't fancy her chances much when she applied for a job at the magazine *Exchange & Mart*. As you may have guessed, it was a job in sales. She knew nothing about sales and, when she started at *Exchange & Mart*, she was several years younger than everyone else, but she thought it was worth trying out.

'They were older, better educated and much more confident than me. I wasn't quite sure why I was there and what I supposed to do. The company offered very good training and, within no time, I was away.'

She was more than 'away', she was brilliant. Despite her initial reservations, she regularly topped the sales league tables at *Exchange & Mart* and won certificate after certificate for her sales performance (she still has them all). Not much changed at home, though: when she showed the certificates to her parents, they said very little and she suspects they were far more interested in her brother's PhD.

By the age of twenty-four, Caroline had moved from *Exchange & Mart* to *Loot*, another sales publication, and had a senior management position with a seat on the Board. She was then headhunted by Capital Radio, arguably the most exciting radio station in the country at that time. She was earning more than £100,000 a year and loved what she did.

'I loved every job I had in sales. Exchange & Mart, Loot and Capital Radio. They were all brilliant employers and I enjoyed success with them all. Going into sales was a revelation for me. I'd never been told I was good until then. I'd never been recognised as successful until then. Or valuable.'

She already earned more money in a year than her parents ever had. It didn't just give her a lifestyle, it also gave her self-respect, confidence and a realisation that she could control her own future.

'I quickly realised the dynamics of the sales world and the possibilities. I worked hard and I made great money. The harder I worked and the better I got, the more money I earned and the more fun I had – at work and outside work. This was amazing.'

Caroline now runs her own company, BuyAssociation Marketplace, which connects property investors with developers and provides both parties with advice throughout the process. With a turnover of several million pounds a year, the company has offices in the UK, Sweden and Hong Kong. As a recognition of her work in growing the company, she received a letter from the Prime Minister in 2015 as BuyAssociation was one of the Fortuna 50, the fastest growing small companies run by women.

'I have always been driven to prove my parents wrong. To show them that I could become someone, that I could be successful. What they said to me when I was young was really harsh but, bizarrely, it's made me the success I am today.'

Her tips for other people looking to follow her lead?

'In sales, your whole quality of life is under your control. If you want a nice lifestyle, you can go and get it. Work hard, be determined and you can make it happen.'

CHAPTER 6

It's The Way You Tell 'em!

'The key to success is self-confidence.
The key to self-confidence is preparation.'
ARTHUR ASHE

Once the structure and content of your introduction are clear, you can turn your mind to the way you say the words. One of the most quoted statistics in the communications world (and among my least favourite) concerns the effect of the words we say versus the way we say those words: only 7% of the effect of our speech is based on the words we use, meaning that 93% is based on the way we say them.

It's rubbish. Absolute nonsense. Simplistic too. Please don't just take my word for it, but look at the research yourself to decide: **http://ubiquity.acm.org/article.cfm?id=2043156**

The words you say matter most, but the way you say them helps too. I'd like to explain how to add credibility to the words you use when opening sales conversations by adopting a tone of voice that presents the right impression. There are two ingredients that will invariably help to form the right impression at the beginning of sales conversations: warmth and authority. I'll deal with authority first and start with another true story from my working life.

I moved to London at the age of twenty-two, and one of my first jobs was working at the department store, Harrods, in Knightsbridge. I worked in the Ski and Surf Department on the fourth floor, though, unfortunately for all our loyal customers, I'd neither skied nor surfed. One fine day, one of those loyal customers had managed to load his arms with thousands of pounds worth of skiwear without any of my unqualified assistance and was now making his way towards me. He was around fifty years of age, wearing an immaculate charcoal-grey suit and a long camel-coloured winter coat. With greying hair and a clean-shaven face, he looked like a successful businessman or senior diplomat.

Once I'd de-tagged all the clothes and totted up the bill, I asked him to pay the total of somewhere north of £10,000. He handed me his Platinum American Express card, something reserved for serious spenders. This was way back in the dark ages before chip and pin, so I asked him to sign a receipt so that I could compare his signature to the one on the back of the Amex card.

The two signatures were completely different. Not a single letter on one copy looked the same as the other. A dilemma. Surely this man was not the same person who owned the credit card. This looked like a fraud. What should I do?

What did I do?

'Thank you very much, sir,' I said as I handed back his 'I'm a big spender' Amex card, followed by the bags of skiwear.

Why did I not question his signature? Because he was a man of such bearing, such confidence, such gravitas, I didn't feel I could challenge him. He oozed authority and so I didn't question him.

When I was growing up, my dad used to watch our local football team – Derby County – every other week at the now-no-more Baseball Ground. Most weeks, after the match, he would be drinking in the Players' Lounge, reserved for the players themselves, their families, the sponsors and a few other bigwigs. How on earth did my dad get in?

'Afternoon, Bernard, lovely to see you again,' he would say confidently as he walked past the man on the door, wearing his smart suit and taking his clean-shaven face and combed hair straight to the bar. He'd made sure to find out the chap's name from other people before going in, and once he'd said it a few times, Bernard felt like he knew him. My dad was always there and he was never asked for a membership card or any other proof that he was allowed in. Sorry, Bernard, you were fooled for years – though my dad did put a sizeable chunk of money behind the Derby County Players' bar over the years.

Now, let me introduce you to someone well-qualified on the subject of authority: Dr Robert Cialdini. His book *Influence – The Psychology Of Persuasion* is the best book I have ever read on sales (before this one, of course) and it's not even written about sales. I heartily recommend you buy it. It's brilliant.

Cialdini's significant body of research proves the effectiveness of what he calls 'Weapons of Influence'. There are six such weapons, and he argues that human beings are almost preprogrammed to react to them in certain ways. One of those six weapons is authority.

> *'We are trained from birth that obedience to proper authority is right and disobedience is wrong. The essential message fills the parental lessons, the school rhymes, stories, and songs of our childhood and is carried forward in the legal, military, and political systems we encounter as adults. Notions of submission and loyalty to legitimate rule are accorded much value in each.'*
>
> DR ROBERT CIALDINI, *INFLUENCE – THE PSYCHOLOGY OF PERSUASION*

When we meet people who act with authority, speak with authority, look authoritative, then it is highly likely that we will believe in what they say. Think of the skiwear shopper with the bizarre signature, my father drinking with the professional footballers week in, week out and countless examples I'm sure you can remember. This ability to influence someone at the start of a call, to persuade them that our call is going to be worth their time, is very important.

So, how do you speak with authority when you're not really sure what you're doing? Particularly if you know that you're speaking to people older and wiser than you and when you're still quite new to the world of sales. Well, it's not easy, but I can help you do it better. This won't just help you on sales calls over the phone, it will help you win a few more debates with your friends, too.

The first mistake people make that undermines their authority is failing to prepare to start calls well. It's remarkable how badly we all perform if we simply jump in and do something new without taking a few minutes to plan. I've talked in the last few pages about having a structure – that structure can be practised a few times. Structure is better than a script because scripted openings too often sound wooden and insincere. By contrast, structure provides a consistently good opening which sounds more like you.

So, stick with the structure and give it a decent chance of succeeding by practising it a few times. If you tried to ski with no practice, no coaching, no help whatsoever, you'd fall down, hurt yourself and look ridiculous. Based on that experience, you'd likely pack up there and then. This is true of almost any new skill, including sales.

With structure and some practice, you're more likely to be ready to say the right words when the person you're calling answers the phone. It's important you're ready because – shocking though this might sound – most people don't want to speak to you when you call. This means that they'll not be especially friendly to you. You will feel under pressure, I promise you.

What typically happens when people feel under pressure is that they revert to habits. Unless your structure has been practised a few times, it won't be anywhere close to being a habit yet. What most of us under pressure will do is to revert to childhood habits: when faced with authority, we become subservient. Subservience is the polar opposite of authority so not a great place to start a conversation in which you'd like to be viewed as a person of influence.

Another key element that will reduce your authority (at any time in a sales conversation or any conversation in life) is to pepper your words with uncertainty. What words denote uncertainty?

'Erm…kind of…sort of…you know…sorry…if you don't mind…just a quick call…'

This doesn't mean these words are banned, but if the first few seconds of your phone call are full of uncertain words, then it's highly likely that you'll sound lacking in confidence. Definitely not a voice of authority.

I often hear uncertainty in the opening lines to sales calls. Don't get me wrong here – I'm not saying you must sound like it's Barack Obama calling, but you do need to sound like you know what you're talking about. When the words you choose are uncertain, you will almost always add a tone of voice that sounds uncertain – the two together are killers and make your call barely worthwhile.

The trouble with those uncertain words I mentioned is that we often use them without realising we're using them. I have coached salespeople over the years and raised this issue with them, having listened to a few of their calls to clients.

'Watch the uncertainty in your delivery,' I say. 'There were lots of erms, justs, sorrys.'

'No,' they say. 'I know what you mean, but I never do that.'

They have no idea.

To be sure of how you sound when opening conversations, record the way you do it and listen back. Most of us hate hearing our own voice, but once you get over that, it's one of the best coaching tools at your disposal, and it's also free.

To reduce uncertainty and promote yourself as a voice of authority, firstly find a way to assess what you actually say. If you hear uncertain words and an uncertain tone (if there's one, there's usually the other), then resolve to reduce them by going back to your structure and practising it again and again.

Secondly, recognise that as you eliminate the uncertain words and stick to the short, clear version of your opening few lines, your tone will probably change and become more authoritative. Some of that will be the natural result of doing it more often and sticking to the same format. How to get better at anything in life? Do it again and again and again. There is no coincidence to such improvement.

But, in addition, something else happens. I earlier dismissed the idea that 93% of the effect of what you say is the way that you say it with only 7% being affected by what you actually say. However, this doesn't mean that I dismiss tone entirely from the impression you'll make. It's simplistic to think that the words we choose and the way we say them are divorced. If we use uncertain words, our tone is likely to become more uncertain. By the same token, if we use authoritative, confident words, then we are much more likely to say them in a confident and authoritative voice.

Authority done. I said that you could also add warmth. How on earth can you do that?

This is a softer skill to apply, a lighter touch and slightly more difficult to pin down. Warmth comes from your tone, but there's something deeper than that. We all know a cold voice when we hear it. When we say we 'got a frosty reception' from someone, we all know what that means. We all know what that voice sounded like, but we're less clear what a warm voice sounds like.

I think a warm voice comes from something deeper: caring. You care about the person on the other end of the phone. You want to use their time well while they're talking to you. You care about the job you do and want to do it well. You care about understanding the customers' needs so that you can match them to the right product or service from the choice you have to offer, or so that you can count them out of buying right now and leave them in peace.

If you don't care, you can pretend to be warm, but it's insincere and will sound plastic. When you care about all the things listed above and more, your voice transmits warmth. In addition, because you care about the service you offer, you say the words like you mean them.

How many times have you received a call from someone who's clearly got your name and number from an old database and calls to offer you something that you're never going to buy? They read a scripted opening from a screen and you can feel that they don't mean a word of what they say. You don't hear care. You don't hear preparation. You don't hear warmth. And it kills any interest you have in their call.

Once you start coldly, it's almost impossible to go back to warmth. It's very difficult to teach warmth because, without care, it can't exist. But you can consciously add warmth if you do care.

Remember that caring element as we move into the next step in the structure of great sales conversations: asking questions. It's the most important part of the conversation and where all really great salespeople spend most of their time and energy. Earning the right to speak gives you the chance to ask the questions.

BUSINESS LEADER PROFILE

Nicola Robinson

Shy academic becomes Sales Director of the Year

Nicky Robinson is currently UK and International Sales Director for Kettle Foods Ltd, having previously been Field Sales Director for Coca Cola European Partners. This was a role where she was responsible for 320 salespeople visiting 6,800 shops a month representing the 150 soft drinks brands of the business. In 2014, she won the Sales Director of the Year Award at the Women in Sales Awards. Judges believed her passion for the brands and her belief in lifting people with her as she climbs made her the sort of inspirational leader that everyone would like to work with.

Yet if you'd met Nicky in her student days, you'd have found the idea of her winning this award surprising. And so would she.

'I was very much a quiet academic and, knowing me then, you'd have pictured me either entering one of the recognised professions such as law or finance or staying in academia and perhaps doing some teaching too.'

So, what happened?

'In my Human Geography and Business Management degree, there were a couple of modules on retail which had a specific focus on driving new business. I loved it because understanding the different combinations of what makes good products, successful locations and creating winning customer relationships was fascinating! One of my professors said that the interest that I showed in that world should lead me to look at working in retail. The suggestion changed the course of my life.'

Nicky's first job wasn't in sales but in a business analyst role at Taylor Nelson Sofres (now Kantar Worldpanel) on its graduate training scheme. However, after a year, it was clear to Nicky and to TNS that she should move to one of the big brands and she switched to Kellogg's Company of GB Ltd in Manchester, still in an analyst's role.

'I liked the idea of using my analytical approach right across a company rather than being agency side interacting with just a handful of the clients on the client side.'

At this stage she was in the business insights team, but not for long.

'I used to help the sales teams with preparation for their negotiations with retailer HQs across the UK by giving them training on how to get away from just negotiating on price. As I did this, I realised that I could help them further back in the process by first analysing a client's needs and how they could position our products to suit those needs. After a year or so, Kellogg's suggested I could join the sales team and put my ideas into practice by being customer facing myself. I loved it immediately.'

How did a shy academic turn into a star sales performer for one of the world's biggest brands?

'My academic mind made me realise the importance of research which serves as great preparation for understanding what is required for both you and the buyer. I still firmly believe that the best way to research a client's needs is to ask them questions. Needs analysis is the first key step to being able to genuinely help clients.

'Added to the fact that I have always been very curious about people, I became very good at making people feel valued (through my interest in them) and then matching them to the right kind of deal. This meant I built very good long-term relationships with them.'

But how did an introvert type handle the toughness you need in sales?

'I realised that confidence is not necessarily innate but something you can build. I learnt to be confident. I came out of my comfort zone and realised that other people weren't so scary after all. I'd operated with very small groups of people when I studied; I was practically in an academic bubble! Coming out of that gave me an immense sense of

freedom and changed not just my career but also my life. I learnt to become outgoing and enjoy thriving on other people's energy.'

With 320 people under her watch, what did she learn? Her number one priority was to inspire each of them to be the very best they could be. She loved the fact that they were all so different and still believes celebrating differences is key to building successful sales teams.

'I'm sure diverse and broad thinking creates the best results. We had such a brilliant and wide variety of people with different styles of working united by a passion for what we do, a desire to do it well and a curiosity that leads them to be interested in their customers. Beyond those three elements, I liked to embrace and celebrate the differences and did my best not to create a one-size-fits-all approach. I often doubt whether there are any other professions with so many versions of how you can become successful and stay absolutely true to yourself.'

What does Nicky look for in her salespeople? What would she need to see from you if you were interviewed by her?

'The ability to build rapport quickly and a genuine interest in people and their needs. Having strong communication skills and a positive attitude towards continuous learning also helps. Everything else, we can coach them. It helps to be memorable too. If we can still remember you positively twenty-four hours after your interview, that's a great sign!'

And her reasons for why you should consider a career in sales?

'It gives you the freedom to create your own career and to work in your own style. It's also one of the most meritocratic careers you could ever have. If you're ambitious, hard-working and successful, you will

progress. Plus, if you ever want to change sector, every business sector wants great salespeople. And whichever sales arena you're in, you'll be surrounded by masses of energy and great can-do attitudes!'

Yet more positivity and freedom. Thank goodness for those two degree modules and one professor. They set in motion a successful career and a happy, fulfilled life.

BUSINESS LEADER PROFILE

John Pentin

A life well-lived

Having worked for media giants like Newsweek, Bloomberg and CNBC, John Pentin has had an amazing career and a fun-filled life. He now leads the global sales team for a digital tech company selling its distribution platform to serve client-branded content matched semantically against relevant editorial content across premium publishers for record high engagement. Sixty-five global household names from Adobe to Credit Suisse and Microsoft are clients, and they're buying into a technology that didn't even exist five years ago, never mind thirty years ago when John's career began.

'When I started my career, the internet didn't even exist. In my first sales job, there was a phone, a rolodex phone directory and an ashtray. People smoked at their desks all day long! It was a very different time.'

Like so many, John's first steps into sales had little to do with a careful plan.

'When I was nineteen, my father kicked me out of the house one day and said I could come back later when I'd found a job. My mate and I headed into London and spent most of the day in various pubs! I've always loved socialising and we had a great day out. On the train home, I thought I'd better do some job hunting and scanned the adverts in the paper.'

John's first interview was not successful, but then one person's misfortune gave him a shot. The candidate who got the job was injured playing rugby the weekend before he was due to start and the company called John back. He'd got his first sales job selling a magazine's classified advertising over the phone. It was a great start.

'Though selling over the phone is not easy, you can at least hide the fact that you're very young. It was easier to sound more mature than face-to-face which meant the clients took me more seriously! Also my experience as a part-time hospital radio DJ enabled me to turn on the charm over the phone!'

He spent two years in that first job, driving a company car (XR3i convertible), doing well enough to build a team around his success and becoming Sales Manager. He was then able to move to a bigger operation at Newsweek where he spent twenty-one years selling, managing and becoming part of the senior management team. After stints with global giants Bloomberg and CNBC, John now finds himself in one of the world's newest and most dynamic markets.

This is what I find remarkable about John's career. He now sells a concept that's younger than some of the suits he wears. It's a wonderful example of the portability of sales skills – if you know how to sell, then you can take those skills into almost any market. How wonderful is that?

'I've always loved people. Loved talking. And loved socialising. I can now see that these qualities – with a few skills added along the way – have given me a fulfilling and successful career, one that I never imagined possible when, at the age of nineteen, I entered the whacky world of advertising at the Kentish Gazette for a week's work experience with one of their field sales reps. They made it look so easy and they had a company car!'

Apart from the sociability and confidence to talk, what were the skills he learnt?

'They're the same ones I share with my teams now. Be interested in your clients and their businesses. If you can get them talking about what they do and how they do it, they'll tell you everything. As you listen, you learn about their world and you see ways in which you can help them. Also, remember small details. I was taught to note points about their personal lives too and refer back to this information later – nobody does this anymore and I'm not sure why.

'Also, never give up. Especially when you start, most people will say no to you. Keep going. If you have a good product or service, there are people out there that will want to buy it. You just need to find them

and encourage them to open up. People still buy people. Also the most effective way of communicating with clients is still by phone – emails get lost and often ignored. At least now I can appear younger than I am!

'Finally, it helps enormously to sell something you like, something you believe in. It makes you genuine and it also means you're more likely to stick with it when it gets tough.'

It's obviously a career that John would recommend, though he highlights that it's not for everyone. If you're the right kind of person, it can give you an incredible life.

'I've never woken up in the morning and not wanted to go to work. I've travelled the world, visited amazing places, eaten in incredible restaurants and met inspirational people. I even met my wife through sales but that's a story for another time!'

What other jobs give you the chance to be at the top of the corporate ladder for a product that is so new, not even the platform on which it works (the internet) existed when you started work? The universal application of sales skills is rarely better illustrated than in the career of John Pentin.

CHAPTER 7

Conversations And Why They're Rare

'Most people do not listen with the intent to understand; they listen with the intent to reply.'
STEPHEN COVEY

Are you enjoying the book so far? If so, what do you like about it most? Why did you like those bits in particular? What could make the book even better? If not, what needs to happen now to get you more engaged? If you had to describe the book so far in one sentence, what would you say? If there was one thing you could change about the book, what would that one thing be? How would that make it better?

Is that enough questioning for now?

If you took a little time to think about the questions I just asked, then you've engaged in one of the most important steps in any sales conversation, and probably any good conversation in life, too.

Most people shy away from asking questions for all sorts of reasons, yet to become an outstanding communicator you must ask questions of all sorts. Questions give you control, understanding, connection, engagement and information. Asked well, and assuming you listen to the answers, they will tell you everything you need to know as you search for the most important thing in your job: the truth.

At the heart of sales is a mission to find the truth. Once you find out the truth about a person or company to whom you're talking, then you can help them. That help could involve selling them one of your products or services; it could involve you introducing them to someone else who can help them; it may even mean that you thank them for their time but let them know that you can't help them today. Any one of those outcomes is acceptable as long as it is based on the truth.

Too often, though, people don't find out the truth, and their ability to satisfy their customer becomes no more than a lucky dip. If you want to be a successful communicator – especially if you want to do that in a sales position – you must learn how to find out the truth properly.

Shortly I'll introduce you to some simple questioning skills to help you uncover the truth about a buyer's needs, but first I'm going to explain the five biggest benefits to asking questions in a sales conversation.

Benefit 1 of asking questions: uncover a need. There are the obvious benefits to asking questions and some less obvious ones, but let's start with the basics. Each buyer has needs of some sort or another. You don't yet know the needs and therefore don't know if you can help them. There are four areas you need to cover, though the order in which you ask these will vary.

Budget. How much money is the customer thinking of spending on this purchase? This amount may change up or down, but buyers usually have some idea of a starting point from online research, market knowledge or tips from friends. Whether their figure is realistic or not doesn't matter – just find out what number they have in mind.

Authority. Is the person you're speaking to the person who's going to make the buying decision? If you've never sold before, this may seem an odd question, but buying decisions are often made collectively. It might be a child who needs the sign-off of a parent when in a shop; it could be a husband and wife making a decision about where they're going on holiday; or, if you're selling to businesses, the purchase might need the whole Board of Directors to agree. In the sales world, we refer to the DMU (Decision Making Unit) because it's often overlooked. You may be talking to one person, but three other people actually need to say yes or no. To be able to help, you need to know who's involved in the DMU.

Need. Whatever it is that people are buying, they have a particular need or desire to be fulfilled. Are they buying a new car because they need a bigger one or because their old one has broken down? Are they buying a suit for a wedding or a new job? Are they buying desks for their business because they have new members of staff? Are they buying a book about learning sales skills because they recognise every job is effectively a sales job?

Timeframe. Do they want to buy something today or sometime in the next year? The urgency of a buying decision has a massive effect on the buying process, the psychology behind the buyer's choice and the information they require when they speak to you. You will also, at some stage, have to decide how much time you dedicate to each potential client, and you're more likely to devote time to someone buying today than someone 'looking at their options for next year'. However, remember the number one priority in your job: find out the truth. The buyer may say they're just browsing, but they could well end up buying today. People don't always give you the truth. You must find it.

BANT (Budget – Authority – Need – Timeframe) is a regular reminder for experienced salespeople to cover the basic information when asking questions. All too often, these are the only things people ask before starting to sell. Please don't fall into that trap. These points are important, but they are just the beginning of the questioning phase of sales conversations, not the end.

Benefit 2 of asking questions: it makes communication easier. Communication is difficult. Practically every problem in the world is created by a breakdown in communication of some sort. Think about any problem in your life now or in current world affairs and you will likely see that a significant part of it is due to a miscommunication, misunderstanding or disconnection.

When we recognise how difficult something can be, we work out ways of making it easier. Always find easier ways of being effective if you can. Sales is no different. Understanding a client's needs and matching them to your products or services while making notes, waving at someone to make you a coffee (please) and thinking about what you're going to have for lunch is a tricky juggling act. Yes, of course you should always be

100% focused on what your client is saying, but the reality of the human brain is that it's constantly shifting its attention between different priorities. Within that juggling act, if you're talking a lot and trying to read a client's responses to see if you're on track and changing your tack if necessary, then you're making it incredibly difficult for yourself. It is much easier to ask questions and listen to the answers. Then ask more questions based on the client's answers.

'Really, that's interesting. Why did that happen? ... How come? ... What happened next? ... How did that make you feel? ... What did your friend think of that? Etc.'

You're doing much less work. You must listen carefully to the client's answers, but that is easier than talking all the time, I promise you. Once you're good at asking questions, listening to the answers, picking up on clues and asking more, it becomes really easy, and it's almost always easier than just talking all the time.

Benefit 3 of asking questions: it makes people think. Have you ever listened to a presentation of some sort and realised at the end that you cannot remember a single bit of what was said? I know I have. The words were in a language you understood. How can you remember nothing?

It's because your brain wasn't engaged in what was being said. You heard the words, but you weren't listening because you were thinking about something else. Imagine, at the end of that presentation, if you'd been asked to make a decision about something based on what had just been said. I can almost guarantee that you would have been unable or unwilling to do so.

You probably said something like, 'That's a very good question, but there's lots to consider. Can I come back to you later?' Phew, you got away with it and the speaker need never know you weren't listening.

This is what happens in sales conversations when the salesperson spends too much time talking. They may have a beautifully crafted pitch about the benefits of their product; they may tell lots of stories about happy clients; they may paint pictures of the buyer's life after they've made the purchase. But, unless the salesperson is an extraordinarily wonderful raconteur, the buyer will not really be listening. They will not be thinking about the content. The same is true when salespeople only ask simple and obvious questions. A client can answer easily without needing to think.

If you want someone to make a decision then they have to be thinking. The best way to get people thinking is to ask them great questions, interesting questions, difficult questions. When they half answer a question, probe, dig, provoke them so you can find out more. When you challenge them, they engage their brain so that they digest what's being said rather than just hearing it. Your best chance of challenging them is getting them to talk rather than hoping they'll listen.

Benefit 4 of asking questions: you learn the buyer's language. Have you ever answered the phone at work in your best phone voice only to find out it was a friend calling?

'When did you start speaking all posh?' they may have asked. Were you even aware that you'd changed your voice?

What about when you were young, having a conversation with your mates in private, then your parents came into the room and asked why you were speaking 'like that'?

We are wonderfully adaptable creatures, we humans, and that adaptability applies to our language too. We change our speech without realising. We have different codes, different words, different mannerisms according to the situation. We often don't recognise how much we unconsciously change our speech until we use one version of ourselves in an unmatched environment (e.g. work voice when talking to friends) and then it stands out as different.

When I first started studying sales and the art of communication (home study of course as no schools do it), I was discussing the different codes we all use with a friend of mine.

'Nonsense,' he said. 'I just talk the way I talk because that's who I am. I don't change for anyone. I'm true to myself. If you change the way you speak, you're not genuine. You're not honest.'

I had to smile to myself when he became a father a few years later and I listened to the way he spoke to his young children. *That's not how he speaks in the pub*, I thought.

The fact that we change the way we speak does not make us insincere or dishonest. It just makes us human. It shows that we take account of our environment and make adjustments accordingly. When I'm on a stage making a presentation to 200 people, I speak a little differently to the conversation I have later when putting my kids to bed. And differently again when I sit down to dinner with my wife. Then again in the pub with friends. In each situation, I'm true to myself, I'm sincere. Those ways of speech are all consistent with who I am as a person (for good or bad) – they're just slightly different versions of me, changed to match my audience.

This ability to change our language is important in sales. If we use language that alienates our client, it's unlikely that we'll connect with them. By asking them great questions, getting them talking, we can hear the words they use, the way they describe things, and we can match them.

When we say back to them, 'It sounds to me that you're looking for x, y and z' and they say, 'That's exactly what I mean', part of that understanding is based on language.

Quite the opposite happened to me on a Sunday afternoon shopping trip a few years ago. My wife and I went to buy a bed in London. We had been recommended a particular shop as the staff were renowned for being knowledgeable and we knew nothing about beds. We had three small children in tow, and our plan was to spend no more than an hour in the shop as, beyond that time, the children would get bored and drive everyone mad. We knew the budget that we did not want to exceed. This should have been a successful mission.

It wasn't.

We had three simple questions to which we wanted answers. Those answers would help inform our decision about which bed to buy. But each time we asked one of these questions – for example, what's the difference between two kinds of mattresses? – we received incredibly long, technical explanations which made little sense to us. If we asked what any technical words meant, again the explanations were too complex.

Later in our shopping trip, I referred back to the technical aspects the salesman had mentioned but, because his words had been unfamiliar to me, I used layman's terms. On each occasion I did this, he would correct me. It drove me mad. I just wanted to sleep on the bloody thing, not design and manufacture it myself!

A benefit of questions in sales conversations – one that our bed salesman failed to take advantage of – is that you learn the language of your client: the way they describe things. We are much better at understanding concepts if they're described in words we use ourselves. One of the skills of all communication is making sure the audience understands what you mean. The point is not to be right or wrong – the point is to be understood. That's much easier to deliver when you learn the language of your audience.

Benefit 5 of asking questions: it changes how people feel. I'd like you to think back to a time when you shared some interesting news about your life with family or friends, preferably an example when you were with a few people. What happened next?

To give an example, let's say this book is completely changing the way you think about sales. You've been blown away by the change in your perspective and you share this news with a group of friends.

Maybe you say, 'I'm halfway through this amazing book on sales. I know – crazy, right? It's written by a guy who was broke at thirty-two having pretty much messed up his twenties. Then he got a sales job, made great money and now travels the country talking about sales and how it's the most important skill in business. He reckons we should all learn sales at school.'

When you've finished that description (and thanks, by the way), what would happen next? Would your audience be intrigued and interested enough to find out more about this book? In most cases, I fear, they would do no such thing.

Just like my friends when they heard about my interview on BBC Radio, your friends would be likely to say, 'I'm reading a great book too. It's about... ' or 'That sounds like a book by so-and-so. He was an addict at thirty and turned his life around by... ' Experience tells me that the second scenario is more likely than the first for most people.

Conversations rarely happen. What actually happens is that a group of people are in the same place at the same time having a series of monologues. When I first realised this, it was quite depressing. I would tell someone a piece of news. Sometimes I would finish my sentence, sometimes not, but in almost all cases, their response would begin with: 'That sounds like when I... ' or 'I did that too/went there too/felt that way too, and what I thought was... '

Oh. My. Goodness. Nobody is interested in anybody else. They just want to talk about themselves. Next time you're in a group of people in a social setting, watch carefully. Look for the times people show an interest in something by asking questions and seeking more information. And compare that to the times when their brains do a quick 'Google search' to find a related story from their lives to share with the group. It's often only distantly linked to what you just said, but that's all the trigger they need.

Sometimes people go even further with their self-interest. They ask you a question that they actually want you to ask them. For example, around Christmas time each year, people will ask me if we've booked our summer holiday yet. What do I know immediately? Yes, they've just booked their summer holiday and want to tell me.

It's almost impossible to avoid this conversational trap entirely, but being aware of it makes you less likely to turn every social conversation into me-me-me talk. Talking about yourself all the time will make you a fairly boring social buddy. In business, and in sales in particular, it will lose you clients. Do the opposite and you'll win clients.

Listening to people changes the way they feel about you. Think of a time when someone spent time with you and was genuinely interested in what you were saying. They listened, asked you for more detail, asked how it made you feel, kept going and asked what happened next. If you spend thirty minutes, an hour or even a whole evening with someone and, for most of the time, they're asking questions about you and listening to what you say, I can almost guarantee that you will have enjoyed that time with them.

The final – and most important – benefit of asking questions in sales conversations is that you change the way people feel, not just about you, but about themselves.

Ultimately, communication should achieve one of three things: it should change what your audience knows, change what your audience thinks, or change how your audience feels. If your communication fails to do any of these three things, then why exactly are you communicating? Of the three, the most powerful is to change how people feel, and that's what asking questions can do.

Let's consider for a moment how powerful it is to change how people feel.

In 2008, Barack Obama was elected President of the United States of America. The speeches he made during his first election campaign were some of the best in my lifetime. However, barring journalists or Obama's campaign team, if you'd have asked any attendee at the end of each of those speeches about the content, I suspect that they would have been able to tell you very little. His brilliant speeches had not changed what they knew or what they thought.

However, if you asked them even now how they *felt* at the end of one of those speeches, I am confident that they would be able to recount clearly the feelings they had. If you change how people feel, they remember it. Often for ever.

In the business of sales, if we can change how our client feels about us, then we've won their trust and have the chance to help them for many years to come. So how does asking questions change the way people feel?

Let's go back to my earlier example of you sharing some great news with your family and friends, only to sit and listen to their loosely connected stories. When that happens, how does it make you feel? Ignored? Belittled? Insignificant? Even though I'm now used to how uninterested people are in my life, I still find it upsetting when I share something important and nobody shows any interest.

This is exactly how clients feel when they share a piece of information in an answer and a salesperson shows no interest.

When you do the opposite, when you listen and show an interest by asking more questions, people feel flattered. They can see that you're interested and it shows you care. They feel important. I said earlier that you can change the way people feel about you by asking them questions, and that's right. But what you're really doing is changing how people feel about themselves. If you can change what people not only feel about you but also feel about themselves, then you really are in a position to do magical things. You can make yourself so influential that your biggest challenge will be to deliver on the trust they've placed in you to ensure that you treat them fairly and ethically.

If you take nothing else from this book except for this point, then it was well worth the money you paid and the time you spent reading this far. The number one value of asking questions is making people feel important.

Mary Kay Ash summed it up beautifully:

> *'Pretend that every single person you meet has a sign around his or her neck that says, "Make me feel important". Not only will you succeed in sales, you will succeed in life.'*

BUSINESS LEADER PROFILE

Barney Stinton

Pilot to Formula One to sales

Having had high hopes of becoming a pilot, Barney Stinton never meant to get into sales. Fifteen years on and he is working at a senior level with global names such as Lloyds and Blackberry on a daily basis.

His sales career began shortly after graduation with a Eureka moment while he was racing cars in a computer game – why play computer games when you can go and do it for real? Passionate about Formula One and racing cars, Barney went to speak to Joe Macari (racing driver and founder of Joe Macari London), plucking up the courage to ask the question many are too fearful to ask: 'Can I work for you?' He started selling Ferraris the week after.

'If I hadn't asked the question, I'd never have been given that opportunity. People miss many opportunities because they're not brave enough to reach out and grab them.'

Barney urges people to have big dreams – yes, there is a chance you may fail, but you will definitely fail if you don't give it a go.

'It's like tennis in that you're only as good as the other person. If they are good, you up your game. Or, if you're interested and excited about what you're doing, you up your game. Make a wish list and go for it. Once you're passionate about that industry, the rest can be taught.'

Barney took a detour into other jobs for a couple of years but ultimately couldn't resist the allure of sales and came back.

'If you're good at what you do, you get paid very well. That's hard to replace.'

It's not just about the money, though.

'Sales is the beating heart of any business. I wish I could put into words the feeling of closing a sale.

'My career now is fantastic but I'm only half way to where I want to be. Earning money gives you choices – I can pick wine from further down the list. Having financial security changes your view on so many things. A career in sales has given me the ability to sleep well at night.'

Helped, no doubt, by a few glasses of that better quality wine!

As with all jobs, there are tough times that call for resilient individuals to work through disappointment.

'Any salesperson can get into a downward spiral. People can spot a miserable salesperson a mile off, and somehow you have to pick it up.

'We have to feel confident about the person we're going to give our money to. Jordan Belfort's linear approach may work well in some cases but, to be exceptionally successful, you need to go off-piste and you need to really match who you are sitting in front of. You need confidence, personality, honesty, knowledge in the product of course, but the main attributes you need, everybody has. This is why I believe everybody has the ability to be good at selling.'

If you don't work in sales, you may dismiss the relevance of sales to yourself. Even if you're not a salesperson, you still sell on a daily basis.

'When you walked into school on your first day, to make friends you would've said certain things and subconsciously used body language to make them like you. Every action in life is geared towards getting an outcome that we want. Nine times out of ten you are lining up your ducks in a way to get that outcome, and that is what sales is. It's daily human contact turned into a job!

'It's important to really listen to customers and to understand why they buy. If you were them, why would you buy? It's not about trying to fit a round peg into a square hole. If you want a career in sales and want to be successful, it's not about the quick fixes. If something isn't right or you are unable to deliver, then say so. You have to be honest and able to say no – integrity is important.

'If you can do this and you're good at it, you'll make people money and they will notice you. When I reluctantly got into sales I wanted to be a pilot, but right now, I wouldn't want to be anywhere else.'

BUSINESS LEADER PROFILE

Diana Morales

The power of ignoring advice

Diana Morales was told she'd lose a leg when she was thirteen. She didn't. She was told she shouldn't become an engineer – girls in Colombia 'didn't do that'. She qualified as an engineer. When she decided to leave her home town and her country to build a career in Europe, she was told not to do that. Nobody left. She did.

'I have always gone against expectations. Growing up in Colombia taught me to be tough – which is good – but it was also a society that put limits on people, particularly women. I didn't accept those limits and it's served me well.'

Diana is now Senior Account Executive at SAP, a global software company, having previously worked at other tech giants such as Xerox and Dell EMC. She's been in the UK for more than fifteen years and has built a happy life along with a successful career. In 2014, her work was recognised as she won Best Woman in IT Sales at the Women in Sales Awards. How did the young girl who shouldn't become the lady who did?

'When I first came to Europe, it was to take my MBA in Wales. From there, I became a consultant, so my early training was not sales but consultancy. I learnt to understand the problems of my clients, to build relationships with them. To do that well, you have to ask lots of questions and to listen carefully to the answers. Once I had the full picture, I would design a solution.'

So why the switch into sales?

'When I look back, it wasn't really a switch. I was selling when consulting. Find needs. Understand problems. Uncover goals. Then find solutions. That's consulting and it's also sales! As a consultant, I would attend meetings with the sales team and they were the ones doing all the client interaction. From presenting to negotiating, I helped, but they led the interactions and I enjoyed seeing them make the deals happen. I thought I'd like to do that! I spoke to my boss and he agreed to give me the chance. It was the best decision I ever made.'

It wasn't always easy. Sales never is. That's why you're paid so well if you're successful.

'I found it hard when I first switched. I thought I knew the answer to their [clients'] problems and wanted to tell them straightaway. I had to be reminded to take my time. To listen first. I also had to use all my

resilience. At least 80% of people say no to you and that doesn't really happen when you're consulting. Thankfully the toughness I'd learnt growing up in Columbia came back into play.'

Diana also faced a new challenge.

'I was a woman in her twenties dealing with men in their forties and fifties. In addition, I was foreign! I'd make mistakes in my spoken English but, even more critically, I didn't always follow the British etiquette as it was new to me. My natural style is to be direct and that wasn't always appreciated. I had to learn about British culture quickly. In lots of different ways, I had to overcome the assumptions of my clients and prove myself. It was hard, but I had the self-confidence to know I would work it out.

'Asking the right questions helped. It gave me the information I needed and took the pressure off. Next I had to overcome my fear around closing deals. It was a new concept to me because of my consultancy background, but I realised that "closing" was a misleading aim. I had to focus on understanding the client. Once I understood, it was much easier.'

Like all successful salespeople, Diana has given herself and her family a quality of life that she may not have imagined possible when she first moved to Europe from Colombia. But it's not just about the money and the lifestyle for her.

'The most important thing for me was to prove myself, to show that I can achieve whatever I want. I was the first woman in my family to leave home, a daunting prospect at that time. Sales gives you the platform to create the life that you want. I had a picture of the

successful life I would have. That picture was more powerful than the rejection.'

It's a mentality that has served her brilliantly in sales, and she's enjoyed success, recognition and satisfaction. All her life, Diana has defied advice to try new things and to overcome adversity. From nearly losing a leg at thirteen and suffering further serious health problems at eighteen to graduating as an engineer and then leaving Colombia to complete her MBA in Wales, she's a survivor and a leader.

'Every leader is selling. Every CEO is a salesperson. We should all be proud to sell. If you do sales well, you can do any job you like. You have the ability to persuade people to do things, and that's valuable in any world and any job.'

CHAPTER 8

The Provocation Of Truth

'The art and science of asking questions is the source of all knowledge.'
THOMAS BERGER

We're moving now from why to ask questions to how to ask them. It is important to do it that way around. As is probably true with all things, you are more likely to put in place the how if you have a compelling why. For example, if you want to get fit, the issue is not how. In almost all cases, we know how to get fitter than we are now. But if we're not that fussed about getting fit, we won't watch our diet and we won't stick to an exercise regime – there are too many temptations to take us away from that. Likewise with questions in sales.

Before we dig too much into 'how to ask questions in sales conversations', a few words of warning.

Teaching people how to ask business questions is, initially, one of the most difficult things to do because there are so many potential variables. I've found, when training sales teams over the years, that people often highlight the 'What if they say…' problems. There are simply too many 'What ifs' to answer that properly. Then people say, 'You see, you can't prepare for these things so it's best to make it up as you go along.'

Just because you can't prepare for everything, it doesn't mean you should prepare for nothing. I'm no warfare specialist, but I suspect that, when planning an attack, Generals don't actually know what the other side will do. But I doubt that they say, 'Sod it, we don't know what they're planning so let's just rock up and see what happens.'

I recently watched two giants of the tennis world – Roger Federer and Rafa Nadal – battle it out at the Australian Open. Neither player knew what the other would do in the match, but I am sure each of them had made a plan in advance.

For both soldiers and tennis stars, their training and their plans will allow them to make changes according to what happens. It's the combination of plans, practice, preparation *and* quick-thinking in unexpected circumstances that gives them the best chance of succeeding. In our world of sales, that's also true. Prepare for as much as you can and be ready to react to the unexpected.

My second warning is that the questioning phase of sales conversations is a massive topic and I could write a whole book on that alone, but that would not suit a reader looking to understand the basics. The nature of this chapter is to cover some of the basics for those new to sales or thinking about sales as a career or as a new life skill.

Warnings over, let's look at how to ask questions in sales conversations.

Leaving the world of sales for a moment, I'm going to take you to the doctor's surgery. When you go in, what's the first question the doctor asks you once the social niceties are done?

'So, what's the problem/how can I help today/what brings you here today?'

They go straight to the obvious trigger. You're here because you want some help; there's probably something wrong with your health right now, and the sooner the doctor finds out what it is, the better.

'I have a headache, Doctor,' you may reply.

In one question, the doctor has identified your number one concern at that moment. They could, with only that information, recommend a course of painkillers – maybe stronger ones than you can buy yourself. But they don't. What do they do instead? They ask you more questions to qualify the first answer.

'How long have you had a headache? What kind of pain is it? Have you had pain like this before?'

Depending on what you say, they'll ask different questions to probe for more relevant information to gain as full an understanding as possible of the headache.

Now they have more idea of the extent of the problem and will probably already know what the next step should be. But they still don't prescribe the painkillers. What do they do next? They ask questions about your lifestyle. Do you smoke? How much? Do you drink alcohol? How much? How's your diet? What food do you eat? What about your exercise programme? Again, there will be a range of other questions based on the answers you give.

By the end of their questions, a good doctor has a pretty detailed idea of the problem, what's causing it and the best next step to help you. In addition, they have a better picture of your life and general health. Depending on your answers, they may have uncovered some other health problem that you were not even aware you had. If they do prescribe those painkillers after all, they've changed the way you feel because they've taken the time to understand as much as possible about your life at the moment. You feel that they care.

How to ask questions phase 1: getting started. In sales, our model of questioning can be based on the doctor example above. Start with the obvious and then open the conversation up to gain a wider picture of client needs. Questions are partly a process of diagnosis. Just like our doctor, we start at the easiest place: the initial trigger for the conversation.

As a salesperson, your trigger is 'This is XX from YY. You made an enquiry on our website about product Z.' Whatever the trigger or link is, there must always be one. If the client has made an enquiry to your company, it's obvious. If you found them on social media and saw that they had an interest in what you do (they're an HR manager and you offer recruitment services, perhaps), then that's your link. If you're meeting them face-to-face (lucky you, this is a bit easier), then the link might be an earlier phone call or email exchange. Whatever it is, something prompted the contact between you, and the most sensible place to start is there.

In the example of David from the Mobile Phone Provider in Chapter 5, his first question should relate directly to the upgrade I'd done on my phone. The first question typically comes at the end of your introduction, once you've earned the right to speak. The end of step one should naturally lead into step two.

'So, Paul, are you happy so far with your upgraded phone?'

That gets you started. And it's a very simple starting point, I know. Before we move on, I want to highlight the fact that this first question is a closed question (a closed question is typically a question that can be answered with yes or no). Aren't you supposed to ask open questions? Isn't this question too basic with a high likelihood of a short answer that fails to engage our potential client fully?

This is still early in your conversation. Whether it's the first time you've spoken to someone or the second/third/fourth, they were doing something else only a few seconds ago, and now you've butted into their world and want to ask them some questions. You are unlikely to get them to open up with long, revealing answers just yet. This is a warm-up, so get a feel for their interest in your call and your questions.

Simple questions are great for getting started. A closed question is not essential, but it's fine to begin with. You must first establish some connection with your client as they cautiously become involved with you.

Let's use an example of a typical call I might make to a Sales Director to introduce my company's recruitment and training services. To put the early questions into context, let's include the introduction too.

Me: 'Good morning, Julie. This is Paul Owen from Sales Talent, the recruitment and training specialists, and I see that you're the Sales Director at ABC Ltd. The reason for my call today, Julie, is to find out how you recruit and train your sales teams right now and, if relevant, to introduce you to our services. Before we start, are you the right person to speak to about recruitment and training at ABC?' (A reasonable and obvious trigger question.)

Julie: 'Yes, I am.'

Me: 'Great. Have you recruited any new people on to your teams recently?' (I'm asking a question that stays within the limits of the first question.)

Julie: 'A couple.'

Me: 'How are they getting on?' (She's not giving me much to work with so I keep going with a question to find out a little more.)

Julie: 'Early days, but okay.'

Me: 'When did they start?' (Dig for more information based on the last answer.)

Julie: 'This week.'

Me: 'Too early to judge, I guess. Did you recruit those two yourselves or did you work with an external supplier to help you?' (Widening things a little bit more though still related to the early questions.)

Julie: 'We recruited them directly.'

Me: 'Do you always recruit directly?' (No obvious way to open things up yet, but Julie is talking to me and I'm still looking for a way to widen the discussion.)

Julie: 'No, we use recruiters sometimes.'

Me: 'Great. How do you decide whether to recruit directly or to use recruiters?' (This is a bigger question that might open up a wider discussion around recruitment and other challenges in the company, such as not enough staff internally to do the recruitment directly. She'll have to think and tell me more. However, it's also a bit risky as she might not want to share. I have to find out some time, though.)

And so the conversation might begin. It's rarely as simple as this, but you get the picture, I hope. These questions are not yet challenging Julie with anything taxing, but getting us started in a bid to uncover her needs around the basics. Going back to our doctor's surgery analogy, we're still in questions about the headache, not yet diet and exercise.

These seemingly basic questions are not easy to do. You have to do them well and be interested in the answers otherwise your conversation will rarely get started. Once it's started, you then need to open up the conversation to get your potential client telling you more about their world. Only when you know more can you make a decision about whether you can help.

How to ask questions phase 2: from present to future. Let's go back to the beginning again for a moment – to help people buy, we must identify a need. Just asking them, 'Do you need this thing I'm trying to sell?' rarely works, I promise.

To help identify a need, we want as wide an understanding as possible of their world right now (think of lifestyle questions from the doctor – smoke? Drink? Exercise?). What current provision do they have in our market? What's happening in their world right now? Within that answer, there might be some needs that match what we offer.

That would be great news. A current problem identified gives you the trigger to sell your product or service to solve that problem. The more you know about a client's current situation, the more likely it is you can offer them the right kind of help and build a long-lasting relationship with them over many years. They met you, you solved their problem, they're happy to hear from you again.

This is the diagnosis stage of selling questions. Find out more. Ask and ask and ask. We're afraid to ask questions sometimes because 'people might not want to tell us'. We're selling to grown-ups and they can make up their own minds about whether they want to answer our question or not.

I had a brilliant taxi journey to Heathrow Airport a few years ago. As I got into the car – with a driver I'd never met before –

he said, 'Nice house!' as he looked at the front door where my wife and children were standing to wave me goodbye.

'Thank you,' I replied.

'How much did you pay for it?' he asked quite boldly, but I answered.

'Cash or mortgage?' he continued. Blimey. Again, I answered.

At some stage, I stopped answering as the questions were becoming too invasive, but I remember thinking at the time that if he ever stopped driving taxis, he'd make a good salesperson because he was not afraid of asking questions. Never be afraid of asking questions. If people don't want to answer, they can tell you. Ultimately, if you're doing your job well, their answers will help them because you will better identify their problems and provide the right solutions.

An area in which doctors spend less time than salespeople when asking questions is the future. That's because, in most cases, the questions about the future are obvious for doctors' appointments. 'Tell me about the problems you're having today; I can work out for myself that the future you seek is one without the current problems. My medical advice can take you from the pain or discomfort of today to the healthier world of tomorrow.'

In sales, though, this is less obvious, so you need questions about now and questions about the future.

Questions start here		Then move here
Where are you now?	vs	Where do you want to be?
Lots of follow-up questions		More follow-up questions

Lara Morgan, founder of Pacific Direct which she sold for £20million in 2013, said of her early days in sales, 'I quickly learnt that sales is actually about understanding somebody's problem and presenting a solution to take that pain away. It's common sense.' (For more from Lara, see her business leader profile in Chapter 1).

In this second phase of questioning, we are looking for a gap between where the client is now and where they want to be. All products and services are developed to fill a gap in the market. This phrase is used so often, you might not have even thought about its meaning literally. Businesses are created to fill gaps, and the job of salespeople is to identify the people with gaps in their lives. A good way to uncover gaps is to find out the client's current position and the desired future position – can your product or service fill that gap? Some examples might help.

Rahul has a sports car that's getting a bit old and tatty. If you can find ways to uncover this fact, then you might be able to sell Rahul a new sports car. However, if you also find out that he and his wife are expecting a baby in three months' time, you're more likely to be able to help him by selling him a large family car that will suit his future needs much better than a two-seat sports car. You might even be able to sell him a large family car *and* a new sports car, both of which would fulfil a need he either has now or in the future.

Shelley has recently set up a manufacturing business selling high-end audio-visual equipment used at conferences and concerts. Her old laptop is slowly dying and she needs a new one. Yes, if she told you about the dying laptop, you could sell her a new one. But what if you found out that she's just raised £500,000 of funding from a private investor and will be employing ten people in the next six months and taking an office in a city centre location? The business is expected to double its staff numbers every six months after that. You're then not only talking to Shelley about her immediate need but her future needs too, and you can fill that gap not with one laptop but ten. There would probably be a range of other products and services you could offer, too.

Think about the day-to-day buying decisions you make. Most of them are changing something about your current position to make the future slightly better. It might only be a short-term better (something to eat or drink); it might be about changing the way you feel (buying new clothes or having a haircut).

Joining a gym is a perfect example of the present vs future conundrum you want to uncover in all sales conversations. In most cases, people join a gym because they want to get fitter. Your fitness level today is not as good as you want; in the future, you'd like it to be better. Joining the gym helps you to fill that gap and, if it works, you will be fitter, happier, smaller or stronger, or whatever else you want it to do for you.

This simple model represents what we're all trying to do in sales: how's your fitness now vs how would you like your fitness to be in the future? We can fill that gap and make it happen. Every business and every salesperson is trying to uncover the present and the desired future. If you can help people get from where they are today to where they want to be tomorrow – at a price that offers them value for money – then you'll make a good living. The challenge is that they often don't want to tell you.

There is an exercise I have done for years with sales teams and it makes clear the aim of a client conversation. When they've met a client or a potential client, I ask them how things went. They normally give a bit of positive feedback to confirm that it went well, then go into the products or services the client needs and how we might be able to help them. If it was sales training that formed the basis of the meeting, for example, they tell me about the size of the sales team and what problems the manager is currently experiencing with them. They then jump into summarising what training programme we could recommend.

Once they finish, I ask a few questions:

'Who did you meet? What's their job? How long have they been doing that job with the company? What was their previous job? Why did they leave the old job to start the new one? Are they good at their job? How do you know? What makes them good? What does the company do? How long has it been in business? Who are its competition? How is it different from its competition? When it loses deals, why does it lose them? Etc.'

I'm guessing you might have the picture by now. Which is exactly what I want to get from my sales teams: a picture. Tell me about this company, the people, its market, its history, its aims. I want to visualise it. I want to be able to see it, hear it, feel it. You do that by following the lead of a good doctor. Find out as much as you can before you prescribe the cure, or, in our world, sell the solution.

The culture of questions is what I want you to take from this chapter. I encourage you to imagine presenting a summary of the company and the people you've just met or talked to over the phone. The clearer the picture you can paint, the better job you have done in questioning, listening and probing to find out more. If you are able to do this consistently well, then you will have a better than average chance of being successful in the art of helping people make buying decisions – the art of sales.

By this stage in a sales conversation, you have at least some information about a client's needs, wants or dreams. The more information you have, the better you can make decisions about the next steps. In simple terms, you have either identified a potential need and realised that you can help or you have found out that the client has no obvious need for your product or service right now. If it's the latter, then thank them for their time and wish them well. Remember that you might ask them the same questions in three months' time and hear different answers, so don't give up on them. It's just not for today and you move on.

If you have identified a potential connection between a gap a client has and what your business offers, it's time to move on to step three of the sales process. There's still a long way to go before you make your sale, but if you've done step one (earn the right to speak) and step 2 (ask questions to understand the client and their needs) well, then step three is a whole lot easier.

BUSINESS LEADER PROFILE

Catherine Schalk

Learn quickly: three strikes and you're out!

One of the first lessons in business taught to Catherine Schalk was the importance of learning quickly. At the beginning of her career, she'd been given a warning by the Sales Director who'd agreed to her request to move from a sales administration job to the frontline, dealing with clients.

'He told me the story of a young married couple heading off on their honeymoon on a horse-drawn carriage. After a few miles, the horse broke down and fell to the ground. The farmer jumped down to help the horse and encouraged it back to its feet. It worked and they continued on their journey, but the horse broke down again. For the second time, the farmer jumped down to help, encouraging the horse

to continue. The horse trotted on, but he broke down for a third time. The farmer jumped to the ground and, with his rifle in hand, shot the horse dead.

'The lesson I took away is that you can fail but you'd better learn quickly and not make the same mistakes. Mess up three times and you're out.'

This lesson, along with many others learnt in her first sales job with Informix Sales, South Africa, clearly served Catherine well. She can now look back at twenty+ years' success working with some of the world's biggest names in the tech sector. These days, she runs Inkwazi Kommunications, a specialist in helping technology clients maximise sales performance.

'The story from my Sales Director sounds brutal, but it emphasised that you have to learn quickly to make deals happen. You do that best by qualifying customers really well. I learnt to listen carefully to every word they said and to notice what they didn't say. Also, to watch their body language closely; I became good at noticing details that others missed.'

From Informix, Catherine moved to JBA Software and then took her first job outside South Africa, joining PeopleSoft, now part of global tech giant Oracle, in the UK. Once again she had lessons to learn.

'Doing business in the UK is very different. Though there's no change in language, the cultural differences are significant from selling into African Territories. As I'd been well taught, it didn't take long to make the changes. The core competencies were still the same: ask great questions, listen carefully, be proactive and resilient.'

Catherine applied the early lessons so well that her career went from strength to strength, from Oracle to CA Technologies, Hewlett Packard and Informatica. Her ability to drive sales performance in the technology world then led to her decision to use that expertise in a different way.

'I founded Inkwazi Kommunications to help others achieve the success I'd enjoyed. Our mission is simple: to enable excellence in sales communication. From training to projection management and execution, we now design and deliver programmes across the world.'

Having worked with thousands of sales professionals across the world, Catherine has great insight for those considering a move into sales.

'Selling well is not just a job, it's a lifestyle. And it's a life skill you can use everywhere, even when you're not working. You must be willing and able to change quickly, to adapt to new situations because selling is unpredictable. You can reduce the variables by planning well and sticking to processes and you should do that. But you still have to retain the ability to respond, to change your plans because people change their minds and situations arise that can change the game along the entire sales cycle.

'It always comes back to the same basics: be prepared and listen to everything your client says. It's the small details that matter and, if you're not paying attention, you'll miss them. It's your job to build relationships based on trust. You do that best by listening, not talking.'

It's a skillset that has taken Catherine a long way. From sales administration in South Africa to global leadership in sales performance in the technology sector, it's been a successful and enjoyable journey. And I suspect she's not finished yet.

BUSINESS LEADER PROFILE

Royston Guest

Creating your own jigsaw

Royston Guest is #1 best-selling author of business growth book, *Built to Grow*, as well as being the CEO and motivational speaker behind Pti Worldwide, a global business consultancy that works with renowned names such as Virgin and Lloyds Bank. He's a specialist in business development and strategy as well as sales and motivation these days, but that's far from where he started.

Having begun working life as a management trainee in construction, he followed his early career path through a few different companies. In time, he recognised that essentially what he was doing day-to-day in his roles was selling, even though the word 'sales' may not have been in his job title. This prompted him to seek a full-time sales role where he built himself a successful career with a big salary and a company car. All was going well – very well, in fact – but he hit a moment of clarity one day.

One evening, Royston signed a £100,000 cheque to KPMG for some work the company had done for his employer of the time.

'I thought I could do what they had just done. That's when I set up Pti. I went from the corporate world with financial security and a support network to going out there as a one-man band with nothing. I had to start from scratch.'

Whether he's embarking on a new career or establishing a company, there are always hurdles to overcome. Royston argues there is one thing within your control when you're striving for something, no matter what it is.

'If you don't have the desire and will, the skills and tools are useless. Great salespeople are like bouncy balls in that the harder they hit the deck, the higher they bounce back. That resilient attitude is essential.'

Yes, sales is about being resilient and meeting your targets, but it's also important to find a balance between closing short term deals and developing the behaviours that will nurture long term relationships.

'After every no, do you come away thinking, fantastic, that's one step closer to a yes? Most people take a no as a knockback, not a stepping stone to yes.'

So, how do you get that first yes? His advice is that you make the first yes an easy one.

'Don't sell through presentation, sell through demonstration. In our business, you need to feel the whole business. For us, that is often through conference speaking. When people see us and experience the business, they think, blimey, this is good. The next question is, "What else do you do?"

'Impressed by your work, they are much more likely to have a proper discussion about the help they clearly need, which often ends up being a much bigger purchase than they initially thought. You end up giving them what they need, but they'd never have accepted that from you at the beginning. So, make the first yes an easy one.'

Simple, but still brilliant. Make the first yes an easy one. Equally simple, Royston argues, is the differentiation between mediocre salespeople and those who are outstanding.

'Deliver a great experience. You can't deliver a great experience until you understand what business you're in. By this, I don't mean the name of the business or the sector you work in, I mean the benefits the customer gets from what you can offer. For example, Google isn't just a search engine, it changes the way people around the world communicate one click at a time. A bank doesn't sell you a mortgage, it sells the dream of owning a house.'

Sounds easy, right? In theory it is, but it's the daily execution that presents the biggest challenge. It's hard work, but remember – if you have the desire, you can learn the skills.

If you aren't sure where to start, Royston suggests the best thing to do is to pick the brains of those who have been successful.

'I did an interview a month with top achievers or someone I wanted to learn from. Ask them for their success formula, learn from it and incorporate it into what you do.'

Clearly Royston found a success formula that worked for him. Fifteen years after starting Pti Worldwide, he is in the driving seat of his own life.

'You either make your own jigsaw or are a piece of somebody else's. Organisations will always need salespeople and sales equals freedom. If you want to create financial independence and have more choices, sales is the career to be in.'

CHAPTER 9

Sorry, Do We Know Each Other?

'I have never worked a day in my life without selling. If I believe in something, I sell it, and I sell it hard.'

ESTEE LAUDER

Your ability to communicate effectively with your target audience is largely based on how well you have understood what they have told you so far. If you have skipped too quickly through the questioning phase – the most common mistake made in all sales, and in life too – then you don't yet have the evidence or the trust to sell effectively. If you've done it well and the buyer has explained where they are now and where they want to be in the future, then you have a gap into which you can sell.

I'd like to take you back to my four-point structure of selling: EASY. A structure is far better than a script because it gives you flexibility, but if you change it too much then it's no longer a structure. If you don't earn the right to speak at the beginning, then there is either no conversation at all or it starts off in the wrong direction. At the end of the conversation, you need to agree a next step and the prospective buyer is either going to say yes or no to that step.

The Ask and Sell steps can change order sometimes. There are occasions when a buyer wants to know more about you, your company and what you sell before they're willing to answer your questions. So, sometimes you have to sell a bit before asking questions, but it is much better to ask before selling. Why so?

Well, there are the obvious reasons that you can sell in a more tailored way when you know the buyer's needs. You know their language and can use their own words back to them, but it's the final benefit of questions that makes the real difference. You change the way they feel by listening to them, by being interested – in short, you make them feel important. If you fail to establish this feeling in them, if there is no connection between the two of you, then the words you use to sell your company's products and services are just noise. You're pushing information the way of somebody without yet having their trust.

When training salespeople, I see them worrying about their 'pitch' not working. They craft and re-craft it, yet nothing improves. It's because they're fixing the wrong problem. Their pitch is not failing because it's badly worded; it's failing because the buyers they're talking to don't yet trust them, don't yet like them. This means that they're not really listening.

Picture a time in your life when someone told you how amazing something is and tried to convince you to buy it. How much of what they said did you digest? Very little, I suspect. All most people do is wait for the salesperson to draw breath so that they can jump in and say, 'Sorry, not for me, thanks.'

By asking questions first, by probing, listening, searching for more, being genuinely interested in what the buyer says, you establish yourself as likeable and trustworthy. It doesn't yet mean they'll be convinced by your every suggestion, but they like and trust you a lot more than they did just a few short minutes ago when you started talking. It gives you a better than average chance that they're going to listen to the next few minutes as you present your case for how your service or product can help solve their problem.

So, how do you do that well?

How to sell, phase 1: check first. At this critical point of the conversation, before you jump into your 'reasons to spend money with me' pitch, it is essential that you make sure you've understood the buyer's needs correctly.

Language is a wonderful thing and is one of the most precious skills of the human race. However, it's also complex and can lead to misunderstandings in so many different ways. You may well have heard exactly what your buyer has said, but you may not have interpreted it in quite the right way. How many times have we been involved in conversations with family and friends in which someone says, 'But that's not what I meant'?

This is usually followed by 'But you said x and y and that means z!' And so the wonders of human interaction go on around the world every day.

You might get away with these misunderstandings with family and friends, but it can be costly with clients and potential clients. So, before you get started, check your interpretation.

It might go a little bit like this if we were selling a gym membership: 'Thanks for all your answers to my questions, Colin. I think we can help you. Before I explain how, I'd like to check that I've understood everything correctly. You stopped playing sport a few years ago when you injured your knee. Over the last three years, you've put on weight – about 15kg – and you now feel short of breath when climbing stairs. You're worried that if you don't take action soon, you'll keep putting on weight. What you'd like is an exercise programme that can fit into your busy life – probably short sessions on a regular basis – that will help you lose weight and, in a year's time, be fitter and stronger, ready to beat your kids on the tennis court. Is that right, Colin?'

We have made sure we understand, and we have also done a couple of other things that are important. We've just shown Colin that we listened. That's reassuring for him. If we've done it well, he'll say, 'Yes, that's exactly what I'm looking for. I couldn't have put it better myself.' There is a reason that Colin couldn't have put it better himself, because all we've done is to use his words and put them back to him. This is not a trick; we're not trying to fool Colin. But we are using the power of our communication skills to help him make a decision.

What we also do in this checkpoint moment is uncover other needs that our buyer has not yet shared with us. When people hear back a summary of their position in their own words, even if we have got it 100% correct, they will sometimes hear gaps because they've forgotten to mention something. Or they've given a piece of information that is true but not the whole truth.

In the case of Colin's gym membership above, he might add, 'Yes, keeping up with the kids on the tennis court would be great. I'll tell you what I'd also love to do: complete the London Marathon. I probably can't do that this year, but I'd love to enter next year and only tell my family at the last minute.'

Fantastic. We've checked our interpretation and found out a real dream for Colin too.

This is why we do a check before we sell: have we understood correctly and is there anything else at all before we make recommendations? Then we can move on.

How to sell, phase 2: about us. You may feel you're ready now to jump into a description of how your product or service will solve the problems you and the buyer have identified. You can match need, prove value and win their business. That's great and it's where you ultimately want to go, but it's valuable to add one more thing before you do that. People don't just buy a product or service. They also buy into the company offering it to them.

In every marketplace, there is competition. If there is money to be made in a business sector, then more than one company is going to offer it products and services. In any marketplace, there are different levels of quality and service, and of course all companies charge different prices.

I often find that buyers don't ask questions about the company until later in the conversation, and I believe that there's value in bringing that information into the game much earlier. It defies belief that the company's track record has no bearing on the buying decision, so let's make sure our qualities as a company are clear before we talk about the products and services we offer.

Before I show you how to do this, I want to address a possible objection: 'If clients don't want to know about the company until later in the conversation, that's up to them, so don't go against their wishes.'

I designed and delivered a nationwide sales training programme for roofers a few years ago. Like in so many other jobs, a roofer doesn't have the chance to fix anyone's roof until they have first sold their services to the client. If their sales meeting doesn't go well, they don't fix the roof.

In my training programme, I met many roofers and asked about the first meeting with a potential new client, from the moment the client opens the front door. A range of different answers came my way. Sometimes, the roofer would immediately go and look at the roof. Others would have a cup of tea first and engage in a bit of sociable chat about the weather and local news. Some would sit down and talk about the roof problem or plan first.

With such a range of different formats, I asked the roofers how they decided whether to have a cup of tea, a chat or dive straight up to have a look at the roof.

The answer was the same across all groups: 'That's not up to us. It's the client's choice. It's their house.'

Telling a whole roomful of people that they're wrong is not easy, but I had to find a way. I asked them, for a moment, to forget the client's wishes. What did they think was the best use of everyone's time at a first meeting with a prospective new client?

They all agreed that the best first step was to sit down and discuss the problem that had led the homeowner to call them in the first place. There might be a cup of tea involved at the same time and there might be a bit of chit chat, but it was better to talk first and then look at the roof. Within that talk, they agreed that it was important to make clear their company's track record and their pedigree as a roofing specialist so that the client could trust what they said later after they'd seen the roof. Most homeowners don't really understand roofs and are wary of being misled by unscrupulous suppliers. Trust was important.

So, while the roofers agreed that meetings should happen a certain way, they also accepted that a client's wishes may go against that way and the client's wishes should win.

As I had done my research, I knew that the roofers in the room had many years of experience. Let's take an average of twenty-five years' experience to keep it simple. In those twenty-five years, let's assume that they had five weeks' leave a year along with nearly two weeks' worth of public holidays. So roughly forty-five weeks a year for twenty-five years means 1,125 weeks of work. They had spent thousands of hours working on and thinking about roofs. They had met hundreds of people and seen everything that could go wrong with a roof. They knew how to run a client meeting to make best use of their and their client's time. They knew the best order to do things.

At that time, my own house had a problem with its roof. I was a potential client at the very same time as I was preparing the roofers' training programme. I knew nothing. I might have been the client with the money to spend, but I was completely ignorant of how to go about the roofing process. I'd never done this before, and the roofers had done it thousands of times.

So, who should be in charge here?

As salespeople, as businesspeople, we should take time to understand what our clients' needs are and then recommend how best to solve those needs. A quick refresh: we've now earned the right to speak to a potential client and have asked good questions, listening to the answers. We have a clear picture of their needs and have double-checked our interpretation with them. How do we then reassure clients about our company before we talk about what they may want to buy?

A simple phrase to use is: 'Before I introduce you to the options I recommend, what do you know about us as a company?'

It is impossible to separate the company itself from the products and services it offers. Think of the world's most successful companies. An iPhone means something to people because it's an Apple product. When someone asks what a friend drives, they don't say a car, they say, 'A Volvo' or 'A BMW'. It matters in all worlds, from fashion to coffee shops, gym memberships, hotels, cars and technology, even film, TV and books. You watch or read something because of the people behind the creation. It's a Quentin Tarantino film or a John Grisham book or a TV series starring Helen Mirren or Emma Watson. It's the same no matter what you sell: the brand behind the product reassures you to buy the product. But your client might not realise that. It's your job to know how to explain your brand well and, just like the roofers after the training, take control in the way that befits your position as the expert.

If you work for a big brand, then it's possible that the answer to your question, 'What do you know about us?' will be quite detailed. If you don't work for a big brand, the answer will normally be, 'Not much!' Either way, it's probably wise to summarise to make sure that the client has the right impression in their mind before you move forward. Your explanation needs to be short, punchy and clear. The problem for many people when talking about their company is that they want to tell their clients everything. What people really want to know is what's special about your company. Give them the highlights package, not the unabridged history.

In preparing for this part of the conversation, jot down some key points that make your company interesting or exciting or trustworthy. Think of the elements that a client may like and which will give them reassurance. This could be a selection of how long the company has been in business (a long track record denotes security); any awards the company has won (industry recognition proves quality); exciting products or services that have changed the market; qualifications among the company's staff; big brands the company has worked with before (people like to hear that others have bought into your brand); accreditations from regulatory bodies (industry bodies often put a stamp of approval on to companies that meet certain standards). From those key points, think of words that underline quality, professionalism and expertise. We often undersell ourselves. It's partly linked to the negative associations with sales which inspired me to write this book – the last thing people want is to be thought of as over-selling something. The danger with this is that we may not sell ourselves at all.

For example, I could describe my company as a recruitment consultancy that also does some training with salespeople. Perfectly true, but hardly enticing. Or I could describe it as a market-leading recruitment and training specialist with a razor-sharp focus on sales professionals. I'm describing the same company, but one version is more compelling than the other. The vocabulary matters.

Words and phrases like innovative, dynamic, pioneering, market-leading, expert, specialist, inspiring and award-winning work well in positioning your company positively. Different words suit different markets, of course. If you're working for an insurance company, use words and phrases like well-established, fully-qualified, 100-year track record, etc. Collate the highlights of your company's pedigree and use strong words and phrases to bring them to life.

What if you're selling the products and services of your own company, or a new company that doesn't yet have a track record and a shelf full of awards? How can you sell your company when there's barely a company to sell?

In most cases, it's all about you. If the company is you, then the client wants to know about you. Use the same theory as above and apply it to yourself. Highlight your strengths and use words and phrases to give them the weight they deserve. Why have you set up the company and why should people buy into what you're doing? Be confident, be bold and tell the world that what you're doing matters, and that you're the best person to be doing it.

If you highlight three main points about your company (e.g. long track record; lots of industry awards; list of big brands you work with) before you start to sell your products and services, it will be a good, solid addition to your sales conversations. You've built likeability and trust through your questions and you've added credibility to your company before you match the right products and services.

If you want to fast-track to a more advanced level to do the 'about us' section brilliantly, I'd like to offer you a fantastic structure into which you can place those winning words and phrases. Even if you're not ready for that yet, you can read and store it for later use.

Remember that when you're telling a client what you do as a company, the real question they want answering is what's special about what you do? What's different, interesting, exciting about what you do? What most people do is to describe the solution they offer. The structure I love most comes in three steps (yes, I like three-step structures). It includes a presentation of a solution, so let's start with a version of a solution for gym membership.

Solution. At Paul's Gyms, we offer training programmes that fit into your busy schedule. Each one is tailored around your weekly commitments elsewhere. We do that with a range of short high-impact sessions that mean you burn calories and build strength in just thirty minutes. We have helped hundreds of clients to achieve the fitness level they want. We also provide weekly menus that give you healthy, easy meal options to make sure the refuelling doesn't undo the hard work you put into the training sessions. We'll even tell you where to buy the food.

Not bad so far. In many cases, though, the solution doesn't quite resonate with people because it solves a problem that they either don't have or don't yet know they have – the latter is more common than you might imagine. Or they might have this problem but it's not currently front of mind and, therefore, not high on their priority list. It's time to get it to the front of their mind.

The first step in the three-step structure is to remind people of the problem you solve before you give them the solution. Let's add the fitness problem to our gym membership pitch.

Problem. We all live such busy lives now that it becomes harder to find the time to exercise properly without losing time at work or home. Add to that the problem of finding healthy food that's easy to serve without hours of prep. We don't mean to become unfit but, little by little, we stop exercising and eat the wrong stuff. Suddenly the clothes that used to fit us are tight.

What do you think? What happens to a potential client when you present them with the problem first? In most cases, if you've done it well, their heads will be nodding in agreement. They feel a connection to you – *this person understands my problem* – or, if nothing else, they've just been reminded of a problem that they had pushed to the back of their mind. They are now much more open to hearing the solution you offer and, importantly, digesting it to see if it can solve the problem on which you are agreed.

Let's put the problem and solution together.

Problem. We all live such busy lives now that it becomes harder to find the time to exercise properly without losing time at work or home. Add to that the problem of finding healthy food that's easy to serve without hours of prep. We don't mean to become unfit but, little by little, we stop exercising and eat the wrong stuff. Suddenly the clothes that used to fit us are tight.

Solution. At Paul's Gyms, we offer training programmes that fit into your busy schedule. Each one is tailored around your weekly commitments elsewhere. We do that with a range of short high-impact sessions that mean you burn calories and build strength in just thirty minutes. We have helped hundreds of clients to achieve the fitness level they want. We also provide weekly menus that give you healthy, easy meal options to make sure the refuelling doesn't undo the hard work you put into the training sessions. We'll even tell you where to buy the food.

It's compelling, isn't it? The third and final part of the structure is to give people the result. Ultimately, we always buy a result. Join the gym? Buy being fitter. Use my company? Find better salespeople and keep them, increasing your sales and reducing your stress. Buy a mobile phone? Be in touch with friends, family and contacts at all times in all places without breaking the bank every month. You don't buy the actual phone or the talk plan. You buy the result the phone and the package gives you.

Let's add a result to our wonderful new gym.

Result. What this means to you is a higher level of fitness without compromising on work and quality time with your family. You'll look better and feel better. And we find our clients are happier too. How does that sound to you?

I'm sold on this gym and it doesn't even exist.

This structured approach is the very best way I've come across to present a company's credentials. There are many others – look up 'Elevator Pitch: How to do it' on YouTube and you'll find loads of other ways, mostly from American sales trainers. The USA has many more sales trainers than the UK, which tells you about the different profile of sales there. Beware, though – much of the online sales training content is rubbish. However, even listening to rubbish will help you form your own ideas of what works and what doesn't.

If you find this Problem-Solution-Result structure too cumbersome for now, then stick to highlighting a maximum of three main points about your company before you start to sell the relevant products or services. Whatever you use, please note the question at the end of the 'result'. You're about to sell the product and, without some interaction at the end of presenting the company, you'll be talking too long to keep the client engaged.

Every client wants to know who they're buying from before they make a decision. Don't leave that to the end; doing it earlier builds trust, credibility and gravitas.

BUSINESS LEADER PROFILE

Gordon McAlpine

Great salespeople are made not born

Gordon McAlpine didn't want to go into sales when he graduated, but he's now delighted he did.

'I wanted to go into marketing but wasn't able to get the right job. It was a blessing in disguise as what I learnt in four years of selling would have taken me ten years in marketing. I would never have created and grown the companies I have without the experience of my early career in sales.'

BigHand, the company he set up with Stephen Thompson, grew from nothing to a £multi-million turnover and a successful £multi-million sale after nine years. From there, he founded The Sales Club, the professional networking club for leading salespeople, and now he advises businesses on how to scale their companies in the way he's scaled his. He's also written a book: *Scale-Up Millionaire.*

For now, let's go back to the beginning. Not only did Gordon not want to go into sales, he nearly gave up in the first few weeks.

'Working for a pharmaceutical giant like AstraZeneca, I had good training but that only taught me what to say when I met doctors. I couldn't even get into the same room as any doctors in my first few weeks in Edinburgh. I nearly quit. The only thing that stopped me was that I hate quitting anything.'

He was moved to Manchester to join some of the company's most successful salespeople and learn from them.

'It was a revelation. They taught me the real world of sales. The ways to get in front of the right people.'

He took those lessons back to Edinburgh and immediately started delivering results on a previously difficult patch. Within eighteen months, his success saw him promoted to a more senior role and later into a marketing role.

After five years in business, he was getting the entrepreneurial urge and, with a friend of his brother's, created BigHand.

'We had no idea what we wanted to do. No plan. No funding. We came across speech recognition and liked it, so we visited the manufacturer and asked to be a reseller of their equipment, and they agreed. We were up and running!'

It proved to be a winning combination. What was their secret?

'We were passionate, but you need a decent product too and we had that. Also, you need to know how to sell. We had a very good sales pitch. We practised it. That means we could deliver it under pressure. People don't practise selling and they must do.'

Gordon's practised sales pitch and his understanding that you have to get your message in front of the right people came together beautifully at a corporate event one day. The guest speaker was Cherie Booth, wife of then Prime Minister Tony Blair. As BigHand's product was perfect for lawyers, she would make a great new client. Gordon's plans were made.

As Cherie walked past BigHand's exhibition stand, Gordon was talking into his microphone, and his speech recognition kit was transcribing every word he said on to a big screen in front of Cherie.

'As her aides were trying to hurry her through, she was transfixed. Every word I said came up on the screen immediately, word-perfect. Within a few weeks, we had a meeting in 10 Downing Street. "Cherie herself won't be joining us," we were told. Twenty minutes later, she came in. Within a couple of weeks, we had a new client!

'We got our well-practised message in front of the right person. It was a plan and we executed it well.'

Impatient to grow faster after a few years selling speech recognition, Gordon and Stephen found the solution through developing their own software, BigHand Digital Dictation. They continued to target the UK legal world and then attacked the global market.

'That's when our sales growth really took off. As an entrepreneur, you need to keep improving and looking for opportunities to take your business to the next level, and sometimes cutting down your target market can allow you to grow faster.'

Gordon's outlook on sales success is refreshingly contrary. So many think of the gift of the gab or some charisma-filled sales pitch with little to back it up.

'The best salespeople are made, not born. The so-called naturals are the worst! They talk endlessly. Talent is over-rated. You've got to work hard. I've always focused on activity – see enough people, make enough calls, do enough presentations. Cherie Booth's story showed that a tiny company can punch above its weight and win big, high-profile clients. We were really good. We were sales focused. And we were nice people. We delivered.'

Having built successful teams, what does Gordon want to see in prospective salespeople?

'Initially, I look for likeability. Then I want to see ambition, hunger and positivity. Beyond that, there are lots of different elements that help people to be successful. We had quiet, analytical types that we warmed up a bit to help them be good. We had louder, outgoing people who talked too much and we trained them to ask questions, listen, be quiet! What they all need is to be emotionally smart, to tune in and read people and situations. Without that, sales is difficult.'

What advice would the multi-millionaire entrepreneur, author, investor and salesperson have for people thinking about sales.

'It's the ultimate business skill. If you can learn sales early, you're going to have a good career. You will learn confidence and give

yourself a great springboard. I left AstraZeneca after four years and I was a transformed person.

'Sales is a science and an art and you should be proud of doing it. I'm a better businessperson because of sales. It's not even talked about in education. It's crazy because sales is the engine of business. If you think you might set up your own business in the future, you must learn sales. It has been the making of my career.'

CHAPTER 10

My Turn. Your Turn

'The best teacher is interactive.'
BILL GATES

By this stage of the conversation, you're in a relatively strong position. You know the needs of the person you're speaking to. They understand what your company does and how you're different from other options in the market. Now your job is to present how and why your recommendations match their needs.

This is a great position to be in when selling. A client is engaged, their need has been identified, and you have the chance to show them that your solution works. Make the most of it!

Without guidance, you will likely fall into a common trap at this stage of sales conversations. I can help you avoid it from the beginning. The trap is to tell the client every benefit that your product or service offers, hitting them with reasons, reports, data, stories, examples, case studies, testimonials and awards. They will not be able to say no when they hear the many reasons why they should buy. What can possibly go wrong?

It's just way too much. Nobody can listen to four, five, six, seven great reasons to buy and remember them all. They can't digest them. When I hear people doing this, I always wonder if a client ever says at the end, 'I liked points one and two, I'm not so keen on three and five, four is irrelevant to us, six is a maybe and seven is the best.' I don't want to dampen the enthusiastic presentation of a committed salesperson, but you need to change the format in order to give the client a way of engaging with what you say.

Sales conversations, just like all other types of conversation, are at their best when they're interactive. In the *asking* phase we covered earlier in this book, the client was talking more than the salesperson and there was regular interaction. More questions. More probing. Two people were involved, and that should continue in the *selling* phase too.

Yet again, a three-point structure will help you keep it interactive.

Let's move our examples into another world. Investment property is a big and familiar market to a property-loving nation like the UK. Let's say you are working for a company that advises investors of the best places in the world to buy property and then offers them a selection of great properties within those locations.

Having asked lots of questions of the prospective investor, you understand that they have a budget of £100,000; they want to buy a one- or two-bedroom apartment in a city centre location; they are hoping that the people renting will work locally; they want a local agent to take care of the property, looking after the tenants and making sure that the building remains clean, safe and smart. You've checked those details and made sure the investor knows a bit about your company's services.

You could easily now list a whole range of reasons why a particular block of apartments in, say, Liverpool matches their needs well. But avoid telling them everything in one go as that just becomes a brain-dump and is useless to the buyer.

How to sell – phase 3, step 1: benefit. Take one benefit, one way in which this development matches the investor's needs, and tell them about it. It might be the location.

Benefit: 'The location of Paul Towers is perfect for your needs. Several large companies have either relocated or are about to relocate to the new business district nearby, and that means that young professionals will want to live within a short commute.'

So far, so good. The problem is that perhaps there's a lack of proof. At the moment, it's just you telling the investor some information and they can't yet be sure how true it is. Nobody sells investment property aimed at young professional renters by saying that the location is terrible. So, how does the investor know that you're right?

How to sell – phase 3, step 2: evidence. Back up the benefit with some evidence to prove it. The evidence could be an example of someone who has bought in the apartment block before. It could be a report on the area. It could be some data. The more independent and objective the evidence is, the better.

For the benefit given in step 1, you could use the following evidence.

Evidence: 'Global pharmaceutical giant, GSK, and Lloyds Bank have recently opened offices in Liverpool, and a report by The Royal Institute of Chartered Surveyors indicates that 15,000 new professional services jobs will be created in Liverpool in the next three years.'

The evidence proves that the benefit is real. You can use your own internal reports and data if you have them; it's just better if you have proof from outside your company as it's more likely to be free of self-interest.

You have now been talking for somewhere between fifteen and twenty-five seconds; you don't have long left before the client is likely to switch off. So now it's time for your final step.

How to sell – phase 3, step 3: checkpoint. You want to check if what you've said makes sense to the client, they've understood, and whether they agree with your point or not. Or whether they're even interested in the benefit you've highlighted.

The easiest way is to check, of course, is to ask them a question, and that's the final step in this structure. Keep the question simple – its most important function is to stop you talking.

Checkpoint: 'Is that the sort of area you're looking for?' or 'Is that why you like this area?'

This interactive format makes your life much easier as you're talking for a much shorter period than if you'd launched into the many benefits in one go. It also does something else for you.

Different people buy the same thing for different reasons. So, if you have four to six reasons why this area of Liverpool is great and the development you offer is the right match, then some people will buy for benefit number one, some for number two, etc. By giving them just one benefit at a time then asking them if that's why they're interested, you're more likely to identify their main reason to buy. This will help you to agree the next steps at the end of the conversation.

Remember, when in sales mode, don't talk too much. Break things down into chunks. Give clients one benefit. Provide them with evidence to prove that benefit is real. Check their interest by asking a question. Stop talking. Listen. Repeat the structure with each benefit. Try to keep the benefits to a maximum of three. Beyond that, it's hard to hold the client's attention. It's not easy to hold yours beyond that, either.

How to sell: extra tip. Before moving on to the fourth and final step of the EASY sales structure, I'd like to remind you about a friend of mine, Caroline Marshall-Roberts. Caroline's is an incredible story, and you can read more about her in Chapter 5 because she's one of our business leader profiles.

Caroline left school at sixteen, and her parents said, 'You will never amount to anything.' She took some odd jobs in the local area and, at nineteen, got married. At the same age, her life took a new direction.

Lacking confidence in her ability, she didn't fancy her chances much when she applied for a sales job. Despite being several years younger than her colleagues, though, she regularly topped the sales league tables. By the age of twenty-four, Caroline was in a senior management position with a seat on the Board at a large publisher. Caroline now runs her own company with a turnover of several million pounds a year.

'I have always been driven to prove my parents wrong. To show them that I could become someone, that I could be successful. I hated what they said to me when I was young. But, bizarrely, it's made me the success I am today.'

So why am I summarising her story instead of moving on to the final step of the EASY sales structure? Because I want to give you one more sales tool to use that's dynamic, interesting and powerful.

Stories are an incredible way to sell to people, and I encourage you to use them often. Caroline's story is powerful and inspiring, and it's also linked to the whole point of this book: to inform and inspire you about sales.

In sales conversations – particularly in the third step when we're selling – it's important to make clear the credibility of our company. Also, we present the benefits of buying our products or services and, as we've explored, it's better to do this interactively. In addition, amazing stories are a magical way to communicate all sorts of messages to our clients. To be a fruitful sales tool, stories need to have a connection to our conversation/product/service in some way, but the link doesn't always have to be obvious.

I have used stories throughout this book. I hope they've entertained you and emphasised a point too. From my own life story (broke at thirty-two before I discovered sales and changed my life) to how little people listen (the BBC Radio story) and on to why asking questions is fine (my favourite taxi driver), I've found a story is the best way of bringing things to life. And it's likely that people will re-tell your stories. They'll never re-tell your sales pitch, no matter how amazing it is.

So, dust off your storytelling talent and use it whenever you can. Just remember some basics:

- Stories need to be relevant to the conversation – if the connection is not obvious, point it out
- Stories have a beginning, a middle and an end – keep to a simple structure
- Good stories have interesting characters or humour or a learning point – maybe all three
- It helps if there's a connection to the person or people you're talking to
- First person stories are best, i.e. the story involves you or has a connection to you
- Keep them short, make them punchy.

The third step of a sales conversation is about selling through matching your product/service to your clients' needs and, if possible, using a story to engage them in a compelling and entertaining way. As yet, though, nothing is agreed. It's time to move them forward to the next step.

BUSINESS LEADER PROFILE

Nicola Cook

Your life in your hands

Nicola Cook grew up in the north-east of England at a time when the region was suffering.

'It was the beginning of the end for many local industries. The miners' strike fought the changes, but lost. There were many others that lost too, including the steelworks in my home town. I saw poverty and deprivation everywhere, but it was the loss of hope and aspiration that was the hardest to witness.'

Jump forward to 2017 and Nicola is CEO of her own company, having become her own boss in 2004. She's also the author of two bestselling books, *The Secrets Of Success In Selling* and *A New You – the small changes that make the biggest difference to your life,* a highly respected public speaker and a trailblazer in helping fast-growing companies use the skills she's learnt to grow their revenues. From growing up in a deprived area to a successful business career, she's lived an inspiring journey and an entertaining story.

'Though business was not really taught at school – and still isn't – I was lucky because my grandfather was a successful businessman. Seeing what he did and how that changed his life was my inspiration when growing up.'

Nicola's grandfather was born into a poor family and had little education, leaving school unable to write. He worked his way up in the haulage and manufacturing sectors, and ended up building his own company into the town's largest employer.

'I saw that you could build yourself a very nice life if you took responsibility for your own success. In my childhood years, I saw people become despondent at the lack of jobs and opportunities. Rather than follow them into that mindset, my reaction was the opposite. If there aren't many jobs, I'd better make sure I'm really good at something!'

On leaving college, Nicola took an HND in Business and Finance, including Travel Management.

'It ended up being a really good decision. I learnt the fundamentals of business and, by the end of the course, I was ready to work in that world and I could offer value straight away. My first job was with American Express.'

Her friendly Geordie manner and a genuine interest in people meant that clients warmed to her quickly.

'The more they liked me, the more money they spent. I also loved solving their problems, especially complex ones. When I look back now, it's clear I was learning the core skills of successful selling even though I didn't think of it in that way. Find people's problems and solve them.'

Add in Nicola's hidden competitive streak ('I still find it hard to let my kids win board games!') and the seeds were being sown for a life as a sales leader and a business owner.

By twenty-three years of age, Nicola moved into management and realised that it wasn't just customers who needed to be 'sold', but colleagues too.

'In my first few weeks, I set a challenge for my team. They each came with answers that addressed the issues in the wrong way. All wrong and in different ways! Why couldn't they understand? I'd hit my first block, caused by a big gap in my skill set: how to get people to do what I need them to do? Then it became clear: influence them. Sell them on the benefits of changing behaviour. Take time to find and solve their problems. This helped me to influence them and to motivate them too.'

After a decade of successful sales and management roles, Nicola received a call from a friend in need. He was launching a training company and wanted Nicola to help on sales.

'I turned up on the first day and had a beanbag to sit on to do my work. I'd gone from a multinational corporate life to selling from a beanbag on the floor. And I loved it!'

Nicola didn't just sell, but built the sales processes, structures, database and Sales and Marketing strategy from scratch. What she learnt in that time is the foundation of much of the service she now offers at Company Shortcuts.

She's another business leader who learnt their trade in sales. So what has sales given Nicola?

'I always wanted to take care of myself and, when they came along, my family too. Sales has given me the skills to build an amazing life. I live and die by my own efforts. I control my destiny. I've travelled the world, stayed in amazing places, eaten in stunning restaurants, met incredible people. I also had the opportunity to help a lot of people along the way. All through sales.'

She issues a warning at the same time, though.

'If you want to live in your comfort zone, sales won't suit you. If you like structure and certainty, you'll hate it because it changes all the time. And if you give up when someone says no, then definitely stay away from sales. But if you want challenge, you want variety and you want to create a life worth living without relying on others, then come join our world. It's an amazing place to be.'

Nicola's enthusiasm for life, for business and for sales is infectious. I think most great salespeople have a vitality, a freshness and a dynamism that not only affects what they do and how they feel, but influences the actions and feelings of those around them. She is the very essence of my favourite definition of sales: the transfer of enthusiasm.

CHAPTER 11

The Death Of Maybe

'An expert is someone who has succeeded in making decisions and judgements simpler through knowing what to pay attention to and what to ignore.'
EDWARD DE BONO

This book has addressed many myths about sales. These myths are dangerous because they stop people from looking at sales as a career, or from learning sales skills to use in thousands of other jobs.

Within the world of sales, there is also a myth that success is all about 'closing'. Closing describes the time in the conversation when you seek the buyer's commitment to pay you money to take up your offer. You can't be a great salesperson without being a great closer, so the story goes.

This is nonsense.

The idea that the most important skill in sales comes right at the end and, no matter what has happened before, you'll do well as long as you close well is simplistic, insulting and damaging. It is of course important to close conversations well, but 'closing' is not some magical tool that will make you good in spite of everything else you do.

This chapter is all about ending sales conversations well. There are two key elements to doing that: mindset and structure. Let's cover them in that order and help you to help clients make decisions.

Yes or no mindset

What's the worst answer at the end of a sales conversation? Most people would say 'no' is the worst answer, but I can assure you it's not. The worst answer at the end of your conversation with a potential client is maybe.

Let me explain why maybe is such a bad answer.

The maybe conundrum 1: little white lies. Most maybes end up being a no. Once you reach this stage of the conversation, there is usually a degree of connection between you and your potential buyer, and most buyers remain too polite, too nice to give an outright no. It feels kinder to say maybe.

People often say one thing to hide another. It's just part of the little white lies we tell all the time. Someone invites you to a party that you really don't fancy going to? I bet you don't reply with, 'Thanks, but I really don't fancy coming to this party.' You're more likely to say you're busy.

Remember earlier I said that sales is the search for the truth. Once you know the truth, you can either help people or wish them well elsewhere. 'Maybe' hides the truth and that holds you back.

The maybe conundrum 2: too easy. It's easy to get a potential buyer to the maybe stage, but it's lazy to accept a low level of commitment. It makes sales skills and habits sloppy. The lazy salesperson talks a lot at people, gives them loads of information, and then asks them if they're interested, offering to send them even more information over email and asking if they'll read it and come back.

'Maybe,' they say, and the lazy salesperson leaves the conversation happy.

But the client is not having a look and thinking about it. The lazy salesperson hasn't found out what the client really wants. They didn't dig deep in their questioning, probe to find the truth, present their company's credentials or find out if the client was interested. Aiming to get a bunch of people to maybe sets the bar too low.

The maybe conundrum 3: time killer. Even if you are only half-decent at talking to people, if you have a reasonable enough product or service to sell, you can get a lot of people to the 'maybe' stage. But all maybes need to be called again. And probably again and again (see conundrum 4 for details). Your 'people to call back' list will get longer each day.

You will quickly reach a tipping point at which you don't have enough time to give each person the attention they need to move forward. Your time will be taken up handling all the files, notes and reminders for the never-ending list of maybes instead of focusing on the key people – people who would have bought with better qualification, attention and follow-up. Most of your time will be wasted, and you likely won't even realise because you're so busy.

The maybe conundrum 4: motivation killer. In sales – and I believe in life – it helps you enormously to be an optimist. If you don't believe that you're going to be successful in sales, then you're practically finished before you start. The evidence says you'll fail 90% of the time, but you must believe each time that you're going to be successful.

However, the danger of simplistic optimism (that's pure optimism without a dose of reality added) is that all the 'maybe' conversations will make you feel that things are going well. In sales, we talk of 'pipeline' or 'hotlists' – these are potential clients who have expressed interest in buying our products or services – and we'll present these to our managers (or to ourselves if it's our own company). All those unqualified maybes make our pipeline look amazing. This is going to be a great month, great quarter, great year.

Then our follow-up calls start. We can't wait to update our managers that everyone on the pipeline has become clients. But we can't get hold of them. They don't take our calls. They don't reply to our emails. Even if we do speak to them, they're not sure or they haven't spoken to the right people yet. They ask us to let them get back to us when they're ready, taking all control away from us.

We see all these amazing 'clients' slipping through our fingers. But didn't they say they were interested? No, they didn't. They said maybe. And they meant no.

This blind optimism hits the reality wall hard and our motivation ebbs away. We question why all these people have lied to us. Well, they didn't exactly lie to us; we didn't find out the truth. There's a slight but important difference. Conundrum 2 – in which we don't push to find out the truth because it's easier to avoid it – inexorably leads to conundrum 4 in which the harsh truth hits us and knocks the wind out of our sails.

Clients and potential clients need to say yes or no at some stage. It's better to get them to say this earlier than later. It saves your time and theirs. It pushes you to do your job thoroughly from the beginning, finding out the truth and presenting your case in a compelling, concise fashion.

I promise you that it is better to get people to say yes or no than maybe in almost all cases. Of course there are exceptions, but they're dangerous, too.

The story of the dangerous exception

'You see, Paul, you say that maybe is really no, but that's not true,' said Henry, an estate agent in London on a training course I ran a few years ago.

Tell us more, Henry.

'Well, a few years ago, there was a couple I was talking to about a two-bed house in Hackney. I called them and I called them and I called them. They normally spoke to me, though not always. Each time we did speak, it was maybe this, maybe that. Not quite the right time. Not quite the right property. We're thinking about it. On and on it went without any level of commitment. If I'd followed what you're saying, I'd have given up. But, you know what? They bought that two-bed house. Their maybe turned into a yes.'

Good story, Henry. How long ago did this happen?

'Oh, about seven, maybe eight years ago.'

And how many times has something like this happened since?

'That's not the point! It can happen, and it did.'

How many times has it happened since?

'I can't remember any other times it's happened. But it did happen that time.'

In the eight years since Henry's exception, how many lazy sales conversations has he had in which he didn't find out the truth but accepted the maybe as a good thing? How many times did he fail to call the people who were serious because he had a 'hotlist' of hundreds of other people to call who 'were all interested'? How de-motivated has he become over the years because he kept believing that all those maybes would become yeses? The justification he found in that exception eight years ago probably lost him more sales, more time and more motivation than he ever realised.

That's the danger of evidence from the exception. Not all maybes are no, but they encourage you to believe in the unbelievable and permit you to be content with superficial interest rather than qualifying people properly to see if they're really interested. I only hope that Henry, for his own peace of mind and earning potential, has recognised that by now.

Beware 'maybe'. I'll show you soon how you can reduce the likelihood of it taking control. For now, let's celebrate the other answers to tune your mindset into ending conversations well.

Yes or no are the answers you want. Yes is obviously beneficial – I don't need to sell that idea to you. But no is good too.

So, what are the benefits of no?

Why to welcome 'no' 1: timesaver. It's definitive. It's clear. If it's the truth and the client is not interested in what you offer, it's better to know now and then you can move on. Expend your time and efforts on other people.

Much as it would be wonderful for everyone to say yes, you only need a relatively small minority to say yes to have a successful career or run a successful company. Take one of the world's most successful companies today: Facebook. At the time of writing, it has approximately 1.8 billion users. Incredible. And probably higher by the time you're reading this. Yet that's still less than 25% of the world's population.

Why to welcome 'no' 2: prompt to probe. You are far more likely to find out more when people say no than when they say maybe. You can probe when you hear maybe, but most people accept it as a positive sign of interest, when of course it's usually not. However, when clients say no, almost without thinking people ask why? This questioning always gives you useful information.

Sometimes the client will tell you something about your product or service that isn't true. They've misunderstood something you said (this happens often), and, when they explain, you can give them the truth. Other times, they'll give an objection that you can overcome for them. Perhaps they like what you offer but don't think it's worth the price – you might be able to discount that, at least with an introductory offer to get them started.

It could be that they give you a block (i.e. a reason you simply can't overcome) that is stopping them buying what you offer. If you keep hearing the same block again and again from clients, feed it back to other people in the company as they may decide to change what you offer to match what those people want.

Why to welcome 'no' 3: empowerment. How does 'no' empower you? Surely people feel terrible when clients say no.

Having the confidence to get a no rather than a maybe will empower you, I promise. There is something terribly servile about accepting the maybe. You'll feel like you're just hanging around, waiting for people to get back to you. They're in control and you're not.

A state of 'not knowingness' is horrible. If you've ever had big decisions to make, you'll know the feeling as you're weighing up one thing versus the other. What are the pros? And the cons? Let's list them. I get close to one decision then have reservations. Back and forth it goes and keeps me awake at night, a sickly feeling in my stomach. I hate it!

Once I make a decision, it's a relief. A burden that's off my shoulders and I feel lighter. Having clarity is wonderful.

It's the same in your sales conversations. Clarity frees your mind and feeds your confidence. You're taking control of your own destiny – a key attraction of doing sales, by the way. This empowers you, emboldens you and encourages you to do it more. This is not about hardcore 'closing' – it's about helping people to get to yes or no.

So, welcome to a new concept – no is not so bad after all. This covers the mindset for ending conversations well. Believe in the idea that it's better to have a definitive answer than a woolly one. There is no fear in 'no' – it's actually helpful.

Finally, recognise that your job at this stage is simply this: ask a potential buyer who has already expressed some degree of interest whether they would like to take the next step. Would they like to move forward? You are not nailing their hand to a table to force them to buy something.

The fear of forcing a sale often stops people from implementing the simple structure I'm about to introduce. I'm reminded of a client on a training programme when I think of this.

The persuasive magic of the TV sales presenter

Beth was a presenter on one of the world's most successful TV shopping channels. We had spent several days together to help her and some colleagues improve their presentation skills (which were already very good). The main aim was to improve the final minute or two of each TV sales presentation – the yes or no moment.

We explored some of the ideas you're about to read, wrapping up and closing the sale of, for example, a vacuum cleaner. The TV shopping presenters would be talking to a camera and wouldn't have any of the interaction most of us have when we can see our buyer, or at least hear them. My points to the presenters were about focusing people's attention on the next step. I could see, as I introduced my ideas, that Beth was uncomfortable with something.

'What is it, Beth?'

'This concerns me a bit, Paul. Our viewers, the ones who buy products through us all the time, trust us. Our whole presentation style is about trust, about confidence. We reassure them and they believe what we say. The ideas here are based on persuading them to pick up the phone and buy these products now. It worries me that someone is at home who doesn't really need this vacuum cleaner or can't afford what we're selling. My persuasive closing skills might encourage them to buy something they don't want at a price they can't afford.'

Beth's pained expression as she spoke showed that she was genuinely troubled and it mattered to her that she sold not just honestly, but also ethically. It's a joy to work with people who genuinely care about their clients – even when they'll never meet them – and I had no wish to change that. But her unwillingness to help people decide was a problem for me and for the effectiveness of the training.

'Beth, you are persuasive and I understand that viewers trust you. Are you so persuasive that someone who simply does not want to buy a new vacuum cleaner will hear your words and suddenly think they need one? Or so persuasive that their initial reaction that it's way too expensive will be changed by thirty seconds of you saying, "Just pick up the phone and give us a call"? Really?

'That's not going to happen, Beth, because anyone who's not interested or can't afford it has already switched off their attention. The only people who are listening, who are engaged, are those who want to buy a new vacuum cleaner and have become interested through the rest of the presentation. They're thinking, *Do I buy this one? Or do I buy a different one?*'

Of all Beth's viewers at that moment, only a tiny percentage would be in that position and she would only be talking to them. It's her job to help them decide, 'Yes, I'm going to buy' or 'No, it's not for me today.' Each viewer would have already qualified themselves in or out of interest.

Beth said she accepted that. I'll never know for sure, but I think she was confident enough to tell me if not. My point to Beth is the same one I make to you. You're not talking people into something they don't want at the end of a sales conversation. You're helping them to decide on the next step.

Now you understand the mindset of yes or no, let's look at the structure to do it well.

Yes or no structure

Step 1: this way please. When it's time to wrap up the conversation and agree next steps, it's sensible to let your potential buyer know that. You'll remember from the chapter about earning the right to speak that part of the benefit of saying 'The reason for my call today…' is to let the client know that this is a good time for them to listen. You're about to answer the question that's in their mind. So signposting that the conversation is coming to an end is helpful too.

You might do it like this: 'Well, unless you have any more questions, David, I suggest that we summarise the conversation so far and agree some next steps. Do you have any more questions?'

It's impossible to know whether the potential buyer will have more questions, but it's best to get any obvious ones out of the way before your summary. They won't listen to what you're saying if they have questions on the tip of their tongue. When you're face-to-face with people, it's easier to see this. You can tell they're not listening and you almost feel them waiting to butt in with their question. Let me give you an example of this concept.

You're in a room with other people doing some sort of group activity. Whoever is hosting the session asks you each to say a few words of introduction. Perhaps you're all asked to say your name, where you're from and what you're hoping to get from the session you're attending. Let's imagine for this example that eleven people introduce themselves in a clockwise direction around the table, and you will be number six.

I can almost guarantee this outcome: if asked, you would remember more about the five people who introduced themselves after you'd spoken than about the five who introduced themselves before you spoke. Why? Because in all the time you were waiting to speak, your focus was on what you were going to say. You didn't want to mess up. You heard what others said, but you didn't really digest it. Once you had spoken yourself, you relaxed and gave more of your attention to the five people who came after you.

Your buyers will do the same with your end of conversation summary if they have questions to ask. So give them the opportunity to ask them first.

As well as getting any unanswered questions out of the way, the signposting of the end tunes people's minds into the fact that it's time to make a decision. That decision, remember, is not necessarily that they must buy what you offer or say no. They just need to decide whether to take the next step or not.

The next step might be another call; it could be a meeting; it could even be to receive more information by email and read it in advance of the next call. All buying processes are a series of simple steps. It's our job to guide people through that, and they're better prepared if we give them warning that decision time is upon them.

Step 2: you said, I said. Once you've agreed to wrap up the conversation and ask someone to make a decision, it's important to help that decision by reminding them of the main points you've discussed so far. At this stage, you provide a headline summary of relevant content. This a real skill for salespeople (and others), and you can't do it unless you've been listening carefully throughout the conversation.

Let's skip back into the world of investment property to give an example of how this might be done.

'Claire, you said your priorities for your next property investment were: a city centre location for young professionals; a hands-free investment with on-site support; and a return on your £100,000 investment of at least 6% a year.

'We talked about Paul Towers in Liverpool and it seems to match your needs. The location is a seven-minute walk from Liverpool's new business district with 15,000 new jobs expected in the next three years. Big brands like GSK and Lloyds Bank are already there. You will have the ABC Agency on site at the development twenty-four hours a day, seven days a week to take care of the building and the tenants, so it's 100% hands-free for you. Finally, the price point of £95,000 fits within your budget, and the returns in the first five years are 7% a year, slightly higher than your needs. Have I missed anything important, Claire?'

These figures and the presentation are entirely fictitious, of course – please don't call me to invest in Paul Towers. But I hope you can see that a summary like this is a wonderful way to provide clarity when it matters. It's important to include both what the client said and what you presented. If you can't do this, you've not been listening correctly and that's a real problem. I have said throughout this book that sales is based on finding out the truth about a buyer's needs and then matching those needs with what you offer. At each point, keep that front of mind. If what you offer does not match the buyer's needs, you will not succeed. Not consistently or ethically, anyway.

If you've done the summary well, then often your buyer will agree and you can move to step 3 in your closing comments. However, give them the option to correct what you've said. Yes, you've already asked them in the signpost section if they have any more questions, but life (and sales) doesn't work that way. What happens when you summarise is that people often remember something else they'd like to mention. Other times, hearing someone describe their needs makes people amend them slightly.

In my example above, Claire might have said, 'We could increase our budget a bit, maybe to £130,000, if that makes a difference.'

So the summary not only puts all the relevant information in front of the client to help the decision they're about to make, but it also clarifies the earlier information they gave you.

In sales, we often hear people say, 'Buyers are liars', but this is a phrase I hate. It turns the relationship between us and our buyers into a battle, and it also shows disrespect to the people who pay our wages. Buyers aren't liars – they just give information that isn't always the whole truth, and there are lots of reasons why. It's our job, as professional salespeople, to help them understand their own needs – needs that they don't always know themselves when we start talking. Once we know the needs, we help.

It's time now, after our summary, to help them decide the next step.

Step 3: the best next step. We've flagged that it's time to end the conversation. We've summarised the highlights. We've checked each part with our potential buyer. Surely the client should tell us what they want next?

Professional salespeople know their products and services inside out. We take time to understand our clients' needs and to match them accordingly. If we do our job well, we become trusted advisers to our clients. Trusted advisers don't ask a client how to proceed. They recommend how to proceed. I recommend the same to you.

It might sound like this if I was still talking to Claire about Paul Towers.

'I recommend that I send you all the details about Paul Towers in writing, Claire. For your investment, you'll want to see everything in black and white, and I'll craft an email with all those details. It will be in your inbox by the end of today. Once you have read it all, we should speak again as you may have more questions. If you're ready to proceed when we next speak, you can let me know and I'll make it happen. Are you happy with that plan, Claire?'

Remember, we're not asking Claire to buy the property in that call. In a different scenario, a different conversation, we might indeed be asking our buyer to make a buying decision, but I wanted to give you an example of agreeing a next step.

Each sales conversation should end with a next step to which a client can say yes or no. Your job, as a professional salesperson, is to know the best next step for each buyer after each conversation and make that recommendation.

While the nature of human communication means that you can never be 100% sure of any buyer's response to your recommendations, if you've done your job, by this stage you should have a reasonably good idea of whether or not they're going to agree a next step. The point of finishing in the way I've suggested is that you find out for sure. You clarify their position. Here's the best next step. Yes or no. Not maybe.

There are no secrets to ending conversations well. All the hard work has been done by this stage. You have earned the right to speak with clarity and authority. You have opened people up to the conversation with questions around their link to you or the trigger for their enquiry. Once they've started to talk, you've widened the questions to get a fuller picture of what's happening in their world right now. As they reveal the present, you probe about the future they desire.

If you can find a gap between where they are now and where they want to be, you have the opportunity to prove how you can fill this gap. There is no substitute for a sense of genuine curiosity. Be interested. Ask why. Listen carefully.

Before presenting your products and services, make clear the quality your company offers. Then, through an interactive sales discussion, you explain the benefits you can offer and provide evidence to support the claims you make. You might also delight, excite or inspire the buyer through stories that bring to life what a difference your service or product will make.

Do all of these things well and the last step will be far easier. You will have so many clues by then, and they provide you with the content to finish well. Take your time. Keep it slow, and remember: it's your job to help people make decisions about the best next step. Once they trust you, they want your help. Give it to them.

The E.A.S.Y. Structure for professional sales conversations

- **E**arn the right to speak to our client
- **A**sk questions to understand their needs
- **S**ell our products or services to match those needs
- **Y**es or no agreed to a simple next step

CHAPTER 12

So What Now?

A decision I made in 2000 changed my life when I took a job in sales. It sounds a pretty mundane decision to a casual observer, but it started a much better phase in my life. I haven't told you my whole life story as it's not relevant, but I do not want you to think that the state of my life at the age of thirty-two was due to any misfortune.

I was loved and nurtured by caring parents, for which I remain for ever grateful. I was successful academically throughout my school years without being a star. I enjoyed relative success in sport and grew up to be a happy, confident, outgoing young man.

My failure to turn that promising platform at eighteen into a decade of productivity, happiness and the steady accumulation of a few quid was entirely of my own making. It was fuelled by a certain degree of ignorance and an element of snobbery on the rare occasion that somebody said, 'You should try sales.'

I don't really believe in regret as it seems such a wasted emotion; what's gone is gone. However, I am determined to do whatever I can to close this gap and ensure that other happy, confident, outgoing people – perhaps people like you – don't lose their way through ignorance of sales. This is a great scandal and something I'd love to change.

At least 3 million people work in sales in the UK, and yet most people will go through the education system and be completely unaware of this career option. Schools, colleges and universities of the UK, be ashamed of yourselves. Business leaders too.

The business world is desperate for enthusiastic, committed, resilient sales professionals. There are hundreds of companies looking for people like that and tens of thousands of jobs to be filled. Why haven't those of us in business been more proactive in addressing the outrageous ignorance of sales and the appallingly negative view of this world that pays our wages?

It's getting a little better. There are some universities becoming more proactive in raising the awareness of sales as an important career option and a critical life skill. We now have a body – The Association of Professional Sales – that has well-qualified and high-profile names supporting the professionalisation of sales. I have become a Fellow and will do my best to help its work.

But the improvement is too little and too slow for my liking. It's time to raise the bar. You can play your part in making that happen.

If you're new to sales, you now know the truth about it as a profession and its importance as a function in business. Welcome to an amazing world! We're delighted to have you with us. You'll almost certainly love it, even though it will drive you to distraction sometimes.

I was genuine in the words used in my introduction: if this book changes one life for the better, it will be worth the time I put into it. Truly, I hope that life is yours.

If you feel wiser about sales after reading this book but recognise that it's not for you, I'm also pleased because you're making an informed choice. Most turn away from it in ignorance, just as I did. I hope you've gained some value from your time reading and have seen ways in which sales skills can help you communicate in any situation.

I'd love to hear from you about your experience of this book. Did you love it or hate it? Both are allowed. What could have been better? What else do you want to know? You'll find my contact details below, and I promise that I will reply personally to anyone taking the time to write. If you would like to be kept updated with sales news, blogs, tips, videos and jobs, my company's details can be found at the back of this book.

Thanks again for reading. I hope it was all you wished for. Now that's quite enough from me. I'd like to end with some words from my interviews with our business leaders. Each one inspired me, and I hope they've had the same effect on you.

'Organisations will always need salespeople and sales equals freedom. If you want to create financial independence and have more choices, sales is the career to be in.'

ROYSTON GUEST

'In sales, your whole quality of life is under your control. If you want a nice lifestyle, you can go and get it. Work hard, be determined and you can make it happen.'

CAROLINE MARSHALL-ROBERTS

'Sales gets you to where you want to be quicker than any other profession.'

SION DAVIES

'I sold myself out of being poor and would recommend it as a career to anyone. Working in sales is an honour. If I wanted to retire at forty, I could. That choice is such a privilege.'

LARA MORGAN

'My success has all been predicated on being able to understand people and provide them with the right products and services.'

CHRIS BRINDLEY

'It gives you the freedom to create your own career and to work in your own style. It's also one of the most meritocratic careers you could ever have. If you're ambitious, hard-working and successful, you will progress.'

NICKY ROBINSON

'If you can do this and you're good at it, you'll make people money and they will notice you. I wanted to be a pilot, but right now, I wouldn't want to be anywhere else.'

BARNEY STINTON

'Every leader is selling. Every CEO is a salesperson. We should all be proud to sell. If you do sales well, you can do any job you like.'

DIANA MORALES

'I've never woken up in the morning and not wanted to go to work. I've travelled the world, visited amazing places, eaten in incredible restaurants and met inspirational people. I even met my wife through sales!'

JOHN PENTIN

'If you do it well, the rewards can be outstanding, giving you lifestyle choices as well as transferable skills. You'll learn life skills quicker than you would in any other department which puts you in a great position for the future.'

CHRIS TOWNSEND OBE

'Some of the best jobs in the world are in sales and some of the most successful people in business are from a sales background. Providing you learn the processes and get good training, you'll be amongst the highest paid people.'

JULIE RODILOSSO

'Sales is a science and an art and you should be proud of doing it. I'm a better businessperson because of sales. If you think you might set up your own business in the future, you must learn sales. It has been the making of my career.'

GORDON MCALPINE

'We should empower kids to learn how to sell. Teach them to respect themselves, believe in themselves. If they learn to sell themselves, they'll be much better prepared. When selling yourself, think of yourself as a product. Once you think about that and can present that, you have a much better chance of getting any job, not just one in sales.'

MIKE TOBIN OBE

'Selling well is not just a job, it's a lifestyle. And it's a life skill you can use everywhere, even when you're not working.'

CATHERINE SCHALK

Acknowledgements

With apologies to many others not listed below who should be, I would like to thank a few people in particular for my book and the life that created it.

Trisha Mason for giving me a shot, aged thirty-two with no qualifications and a working history that suggested little promise. Thanks for taking that risk. It changed my life.

Scott Barham for introducing me to Trisha and, years earlier, for kicking my arse out of bed one day when I wasn't working. You taught me a great lesson in life that day.

Matt Drought for introducing me to sales training and getting me started.

Chris Brindley for giving me regular reminders of why this book matters. I started it without you; I'm not sure I'd have finished it without you.

Clive Bertram, my oldest mate, for lending me your back bedroom and your support when I was (nearly) down and out in my early thirties. Thanks Bertie.

To all the **business leaders** interviewed for the book, thanks for your support, your time and your insight. I was inspired by every one of you, even though some interviews didn't make it into the final edited version. Thanks to: Nick Porter, Catherine Schalk, Mike Tobin OBE, Charles McLachlan, Gordon

McAlpine, Julie Rodilosso, Philippa Myall-Chance, Chris Townsend OBE, John Pentin, Diana Morales, Barney Stinton, Nicky Robinson, Zhanna Martyniuk, Chris Brindley, Lara Morgan, Sion Davies, Caroline Marshall-Roberts, Mike Birch, Royston Guest and Marcus Vassiliou.

Louis Mann and Danielle Raymont – thanks for the support, the proof-reading, the honest feedback and for putting up with me at work while I laboured on the book.

Mum and Dad – thanks for the support and love from the day I was born.

Mark and Johnny – perfect brothers are a combination of being a pain in the arse, great fun and showing loyalty when it matters. You've delivered on all three.

Claire Owen – I fell in love with you when I was broke and hopeless. Now, at least, I'm no longer broke. Thanks for your support since 10 March 2000. I love you.

Finally, I'd like to thank my children **Samuel, Alfie and Violet** – you make me smile every day and inspire me to be a better man. Your interest in my book has warmed my heart. I love you now and for ever.

The Author

Since his discovery of sales at the age of thirty-two, Paul has spent fifteen years developing market-leading services alongside successful sales teams. In 2011, he founded Sales Talent, a company specialising in the recruitment and training of salespeople. In 2012, as part of his mission to re-sell sales, he launched the nationwide skills programme – *Let's get Britain selling!* © – to introduce thousands more people to the world of sales. It has been delivered at over forty universities across the UK.

Having grown up in Derby, he now lives in London with his wife, Claire, and three children, Samuel, Alfie and Violet. He loves sport, literature, business, politics, stand-up comedy and chewing the fat with friends and family over a beer and a bite to eat.

Contact details:

www.salestalentuk.com
p.owen@salestalentuk.com

Further Reading and Resources (including free download)

If you liked this book and would like to read more about sales as a business skill or a career, here are a few books I've read that you will probably like too.

To Sell is Human: The Surprising Truth About Persuading, Convincing, and Influencing Others by Daniel Pink

Influence: The Psychology of Persuasion by Dr Robert Cialdini

How To Win Friends and Influence People by Dale Carnegie

Life's A Pitch: What The World's Best Sales People Can Teach Us All by Philip Delves Broughton

FREE DOWNLOAD OFFER

If you'd like to have your own copy of our E.A.S.Y. sales template to help with your sales conversations or to help train your own teams, simply email me direct on p.owen@salestalentuk.com and I will send you a download link. The E.A.S.Y. sales template includes prompt notes from me as well as room to make your own notes. It's always better to sell using your own words, not mine.